T5-BPY-554

The Global Financial Structure in Transition

Consequences for International Finance and Trade

Edited by
Joel McClellan
In association with the
Global Interdependence Center

Lexington Books
D.C. Heath and Company/Lexington, Massachusetts/Toronto

Library of Congress Cataloging in Publication Data

Main entry under title:
  The Global financial structure in transition.

  Includes index.
  1. International finance—Congresses. 2. International economic
relations—Congresses. 3. Debts, External—Developing countries—Congresses.
4. Developing countries—Economic policy—Congresses. 5. Steel industry and
trade—Congresses. I. McClellan, Joel. II. Global Interdependence Center.
HG3881.G575 1985   . 332'.042   84-28867
ISBN 0-669-09581-8 (alk. paper)

Copyright © 1985 by D.C. Heath and Company

All rights reserved. No part of this publication may be reproduced or transmitted in
any form or by any means, electronic or mechanical, including photocopy, recording, or
any information storage or retrieval system, without permission in writing from the
publisher.

Published simultaneously in Canada
Printed in the United States of America on acid-free paper
International Standard Book Number: 0-669-09581-8
Library of Congress Catalog Card Number: 84-28867

The Global
Financial Structure
in Transition

δδ1
ā575
98ī

Contents

263366

Tables

Preface

It is a very risky business to edit a book on international monetary issues. Each morning participants in this sphere apprehensively tear open the wrapper of the *Financial Times* to see if everything is still in place. Some days are better than others. The most unsettling time is toward the end of each quarter (earlier and earlier it seems) when the bankers and debtors begin playing their quarterly game of chicken under the hardly benevolent eyes of the helpless International Monetary Fund (IMF) referee.

Thus, I consider myself lucky if the debt problem and other serious international financial issues remain when this book appears. I will not be the only lucky one, however, because if the problem is still with us, almost all actors on the international financial scene can consider themselves lucky to have avoided the even more serious quick solutions that are looming over the horizon and entail the collapse of the entire international monetary system.

Global interdependence is a rather abstract concept that is paid lip service in most international forums and by most international actors in the world economy. However, many of those same actors have often turned around and operated as if they were autonomous forces fully in control of their own destinies. Few participants in domestic economic systems even acknowledge the idea of international interdependences, as is attested to by the many beggar-my-neighbor policies that are being pushed by labor and management in many of the industrialized countries.

International economic interdependence has recently become much more apparent during the world economic crises of the past decade, and the new awareness is above all due to the explosive growth of international financial markets. Not only do bankers and international traders worry about foreign interest rates and wonder about the over- or undervaluation of foreign moneys, but also workers in Toledo, Ohio, and Buenos Aires are keenly aware that movements in international interest and exchange rates affect not only the retail prices they pay but also the very existence of their jobs. Perhaps the best understanding of what an undervalued yen really means can be found in Detroit, in the industrial heartland of the United States.

It is not as if there were no past lessons. Older generations were acutely aware that disregard of global interdependence in the 1930s seriously exacerbated the economic depression, and they gave their support at some cost to economic sovereignty to their governments as they built the Bretton Woods system.

However, memories are short, and for the most part, everything was peaceful on the international monetary front during several postwar decades for most people in the industrialized countries. Those countries came to expect stable exchange rates and were soon lulled into forgetting that domestic policies abroad could have some impact on their lives. Vietnam focused people's attention on war, and few reflected on the cost of war until its conclusion. President DeGaulle was virtually the only leader in the industrial countries who fumed openly about the international economic costs of the "U.S." war. In those days of fixed exchange rates and regulated interest rates, international bankers and traders, and some academics, were fully aware of the international webs that tied national economies together. Even when the fixed rate system fell apart and the United States detached itself from gold, few people not in the financial business gave it even a second thought as having any effect on their lives.

However, such an awareness came suddenly, with a shock to the populations of the industrialized countries, when a few rather exotic countries decided to band together and raise oil prices. People were suddenly lining up for that mundane commodity running their cars, old people were faced with the shrinking real value of their savings, and hale, hearty, and willing workers lost their jobs.

There are many dimensions to global economic interdependence. On one front, the geographical interdependence of trade that was brought home by the oil price rise has for a long time been obvious to consumers as they buy goods from the four corners of the world. On another front, the rapid expansion of the Eurocurrency markets and the consequent crumbling of banking regulations and exchange controls have encouraged the development of a huge and volatile world financial market that insomniacs can play virtually 24 hours a day and that transparently links domestic fiscal and financial policies in ways that were seldom apparent before.

However, one area of interdependence has largely been ignored even by those most active in the international economy—that is, the link between international trade and international finance. If, as Robert Gottschalk contends in chapter 18, bankers are ignorant about trade policy, the contrary is also true that traders in the past have paid little attention to what was going on in international financial markets. Even in much of the university world, courses about international economics tend not to link the two areas, with macroeconomists tending the patch of international finance and microeconomists taking on the so-called pure theory of trade.

Thus, it is particularly welcome that Fritz Leutwiler's keynote paper (chapter 1) stresses the point that "international indebtedness and world trade are narrowly linked." This point was continually stressed throughout the Fifth International Monetary and Trade Conference both by speakers and in the floor discussion. One international trader raised the issue in very practical terms: "What avenues do we have as exporters, as providers of product, to deal with the countries that are in difficulties . . . ? How do we get our money?" Though no easy answers were forthcoming from the group, at least the issue was raised and discussed among traders and international bankers from both the private and public sectors. In the past, as is noted by Mr. Gottschalk, bankers were loaning money to Third World industries for the development of exports that could not be sold in the industrialized countries because of domestic legislation.

One of the distinctive features of the conferences organized by the Global Interdependence Center is the bringing together of international policymakers and private sector practitioners. Participants in the rapidly growing, highly volatile international financial markets are having to cope with the day-to-day effects of high interest rates, overvalued exchange rates, and budget deficits. Their very practical, often short-term view is reflected in the chapters presented here that not only describe how they have come to cope with the present unstable situation in the international economy but also offer some strong criticism of the policymakers. One is hard put to find someone in the private sector who is not worried about the deficit, and statistics are offered to support the belief the budget deficit is absorbing world savings and crowding out private investment. However, these people tend to pay little attention to the longer-term problems of international trade.

The contributions from the policymakers, though no less critical, tend to concentrate less on coping with the present instabilities than on the longer-term problems facing the international monetary system. In particular, widespread concern is expressed about trade and protectionism. All central bankers discuss the problem in their chapters, and Mr. Leutwiler, among others, devotes an important section of his chapter to the issue, stressing that while developing countries need free trade to pay their debts, the industrialized countries will benefit from the more efficient policies of trade liberalization.

The Global Interdependence Center felt that protectionism was such an important issue that it scheduled for the first time a session entirely devoted to a case study of a single industry. The steel industry faces difficult problems in both the industrialized and developing countries, and the contributions of Mr. Pratini (chapter 11) from Brazil and Mr. Boni (chapter 17) from the United States raise the important issues of protectionism and restructuring. The case study highlights the dilemma faced by debtor countries like Brazil who need to expand their industrial exports if only to service their debt but who find themselves being increasingly kept out of markets in the industrialized countries. Opposition to U.S. protectionism comes not only from the developing countries but also from Europeans who have a restructuring problem of their own. Perhaps one thing that is missing from the steel industry chapter is the implications of the successful restructuring of the U.S. industry on Third World steel exporters.

The world of finance traditionally has little sympathy for debtors. Individuals were held responsible for the debts they incurred and paid the consequences for unwise borrowing. In the case of corporations, shareholders were aware that they could lose their investment if the corporation was unable to service its debts. It served management right if they lost their jobs, and while labor that was laid off by a bankruptcy was in a sense an innocent sufferer (unless it had built up wages to an uneconomical level), most people assumed that they could move into other work after a temporary setback in living standards.

The case of the sovereign borrower was different. In spite of many historical examples, it was assumed that countries would not go bankrupt and default on their loans. At first, bankers insisted that the debt problem in the developing countries was a liquidity problem, and when it became clear that short-term loans would not be enough, they grasped the magic wand of adjustment. If adjustment would prevent bankruptcy, then bankers could still claim that there was not an insolvency problem. However, bankruptcy has a cathartic effect in the sense of wiping the slate clean. Adjustment spreads widely a sharp and lingering pain, particularly among segments of the population who feel little responsibility for the debt problem in the first place. The world financial community has been slow to realize this aspect of global interdependence.

Thus, Part IV, dealing with adjustment policies in the developing countries, brings home to many participants the dangers ahead in the debtor countries. The case studies of Brazil and Mexico (chapters 11 and 12) fill out the abstract concept of adjustment, giving a glimpse of the human costs of the much lauded adjustment policies of those countries. The tremendous costs to future development of a continuing net capital outflow are stressed.

No simple solutions are offered in this book; most participants seem to place hope in continuing to muddle through. The two chapters devoted to future prospects (chapters 20 and 21) both reject radical solutions like a new Bretton Woods system. Both chapters stress the need to strengthen international institutions like the IMF and indicate the need for the developing countries to put their houses in order. Mr. McNamar is preoccupied with the short term, calling for continued private bank lending and the need of increased bridging finance, while Mr. Hormats discusses the need for increased lending for structural adjustment, particularly by the World Bank. He adds that one possible answer would be a slow opening up of the developing countries to direct foreign investment. The book carefully avoids raising the issue of what might be done if developing countries begin defaulting.

An essential part of Global Interdependence Center conferences is the discussion periods. Participants in this section are almost equally as distinguished as the speakers, which makes for lively discussion and a wide interchange of ideas and experience. It is thus appropriate to conclude this book with a chapter written by one of the participants after the conference. Mr. Herman integrates speeches, discussion, and his personal experience in relating the conference to the future prospects of the developing countries. While his is a personal view, it provides an excellent example of the spirit of cross-fertilization and high level discussion that has come to characterize the International Monetary and Trade Conferences.

Finally, the publication of the conference proceedings enables the Global Interdependence Center to disseminate the high-level discussions of the conference to a much wider audience. This would not have been possible without a generous grant from the American Express Foundation.

Part I
Introduction

1
International Indebtedness and World Trade

Fritz Leutwiler

International indebtedness and world trade are narrowly linked. In fact, the origins of the current debt problem can be found to a large extent in recent developments in international trade. At the same time, there is little doubt that the best hopes to resolve the crisis lie with world trade.

That international indebtedness and world trade are somehow related should be obvious to everyone. Only countries engaged in foreign trade can accumulate foreign assets or liabilities. Closed economies, if there are any, do not have a debt problem. Ever since David Ricardo, economists have been convinced that international trade benefits all participating nations. By exploiting their comparative advantages, trading nations can increase their incomes and, if they so choose, consume more of all goods. International trade also tends to lead to more economic stability by dampening the impact of domestic shocks, although it does expose the domestic economy to foreign developments. International trade allows for transfers of wealth between nations. Countries can lend to the rest of the world by running current account surpluses, or they can borrow by running deficits. This additional degree of freedom can be precious when making intertemporal decisions or for reducing fluctuations. At the same time, such freedom presents a risk if it leads to excesses.

While international trade provides the setting for the debt problem, it appears that recent trade developments triggered it. The debt problem is largely due to the unfavorable evolution of the terms of trade of non-oil-exporting developing nations over the last decade, particularly since 1979. Of course, many other factors have played a role as well: poor domestic economic policies, unfavorable demographic trends, towering interest rates, just to name some of the most obvious. However, the deterioration of the terms of trade has perhaps been the single most important factor.

Oil-importing nations have experienced sharp increases in their import prices in the aftermath of the two oil shocks of the 1970s.

Moreover, many of the same countries have been hurt by the collapse of commodity prices, and by export prices in general, during the recent recession, the severest one since the 1930s.

The adverse change in the terms of trade has resulted in a sharp and unexpected drop in the real income of non-oil-exporting nations, and it has induced some of them to rely heavily on foreign borrowing to maintain previous levels of domestic absorption. This reliance is particularly apparent for less developed countries (LDCs) that are subject to sharp demographic pressures. Between 1978 and 1980, the annual current account deficits of non-oil-exporting developing nations increased by approximately $40 billion. This figure matches quite closely the increase in their oil bill. In the case of middle income and newly industrialized countries, much of the gap was financed by international bank lending.

The two oil shocks caused a gigantic redistribution of world income from industrialized nations and most of the Third World to OPEC (Organization of Petroleum Exporting Countries) countries. Consumption adjusted slowly everywhere, and the last decade saw a substantial transfer of wealth to oil-exporting nations. The newly acquired wealth, in turn, was used largely to finance the current account deficits of oil-importing nations through the intermediary of the Western banking system. The recycling problem was thus taken care of in the simplest possible way; the savings of OPEC countries were matched by the dissavings of oil-importing nations. There was no pressing need, it seemed, for any real adjustments. Large debts were accumulated, often to finance current consumption rather than to set the foundations for future economic growth. Resources have been wasted, and economic mismanagement—and corruption in some cases—have taken their toll.

To be fair one must recognize, however, that many non-oil-exporting LDCs have achieved very respectable rates of growth throughout the 1970s and until as late as 1981. This new growth indicates that many resources were indeed put to productive use and that not all debt was imprudently acquired. Unfortunately, gross national product (GNP) growth has clearly not been sufficient to keep pace with the bulging foreign debts.

The terms of trade of LDCs deteriorated further as a result of the collapse of their export markets. The recession from which the United States and other industrialized nations are just emerging has been accompanied by a sharp reduction in demand for LDC exports, which has had a substantial negative impact on both prices and quantitites. Thus, LDC export revenues have fallen significantly. The prices of several important commodities remain depressed, and this hurts many middle and low income countries that rely heavily on exports of a small number of raw materials. Even newly industrialized countries that export a variety of manufactured and semimanufactured goods have seen their export prospects decline as demand has fallen and protectionism has risen in the Western world.

The crisis has been exacerbated by the explosion of interest rates. During the 1970s, an increasing share of bank debt came to carry floating interest rates that made the debtor countries particularly vulnerable to upswings in interest rates. Interest payments increased dramatically at the turn of the decade as the London Inter-Bank Offer Rate (LIBOR) rose to an average close to 17 percent during 1981. The interest payments of Mexico, Brazil, Argentina, and South Korea nearly quadrupled between 1978 and 1981 to reach $23 billion in the latter year.

The three events—(1) the increase in oil prices, (2) the collapse of export markets, and (3) the explosion of interest rates—had a direct impact on the current accounts of the LDCs. Their combined effect has been disastrous. The increase in oil prices is likely to be permanent and requires real adjustments. The other two shocks are more cyclical in nature, and one might think that they could be weathered out. However, their sheer size and timing are such that they cannot be overcome within a relatively short period of time.

The current situation is sometimes described as a liquidity crisis as opposed to a solvency crisis. It is certainly true that there have been noticeable elements of a liquidity squeeze, particularly in the second half of 1982. The Bank for International Settlements (BIS) warned against the abrupt halt in new lending to non-OPEC developing countries. Nevertheless, net outstanding bank debt to these countries actually fell during the third quarter of 1982, and subsequent increases were almost entirely due to unspontaneous bank credits associated with International Monetary Fund (IMF) lending packages. The liquidity squeeze is related, in part, to the cyclical factors already described, but the roots of the problem lie far deeper. The current crisis will not be resolved with the help of rescheduling and new credits alone. What is also essential is a fundamental change in the economic policies of debtor countries, particularly fiscal and monetary policies.

In the future, indebted countries will have to live within their means. The adjustments are long overdue. However, the existing debts cannot be repaid in the foreseeable future, and indeed there is no need for it, just like there is no need for the net debts of the U.S. government, corporate, or household sectors ever to be paid back. Nobody expects the sum of outstanding mortgages in the United States to start declining and eventually melt away. It is quite natural for a country in the early stages of its development to be indebted since it may lack the resources needed to exploit existing opportunities. Even industrialized nations such as

Canada and Australia, relatively labor and capital scarce but well endowed with natural resources, need outside help to tap their development potential.

There is nothing wrong with a country being indebted. The debt may even be allowed to grow over time, but it must remain manageable; that is, it must bear some relationship to the size of the debtor's economy and, most important, to its capacity to service it. It is noteworthy that these countries that show the worst relation between debt service and exports have run into serious payment difficulties. Third World debts will continue to grow in the future, but their size must come down relative to the scale of these economies. World inflation and future decreases in interest rates will reduce the real burden of existing debts. Economic recovery and sustained growth will decrease the relative size of indebtedness.

While the roots of the debt problem are largely of a commercial nature, there is little doubt that international trade offers the best hope for the future. Closed economies can offer no quarantee to their foreign creditors. It has long been established that international trade provides a strong stimulus for domestic economic growth. Furthermore, unless the debtor countries manage to achieve rates of growth in excess of real interest rates, they will have to run trade surpluses to bring down their debts relative to their incomes.

What the industrialized world must offer the indebted countries is time and a setting favorable to international trade. LDCs must expand their exports. They need larger export revenues to service their debts and to finance their development. To reduce their vulnerability to cyclical movements in commodity prices, they must diversify their production. Their best solution often lies with semimanufactured and manufactured goods. Diversification must take place with export markets in mind. Efforts directed at import substitution under the umbrella of high local tariffs only lead to a misallocation of resources.

Since the bulk of Third World trade is with Western industrialized nations, it is clear where responsibilities lie. Protectionism seems to be on the rise throughout the world. This trend must be reversed, however. Based on their own self-interest, the industrialized countries must give developing nations a fair chance to expand their exports. After all, if the industrialized nations cannot be paid in cash, why refuse to be paid in kind?

Few obstacles exist to free trade in raw materials and tropical agricultural products (with the exception of sugar). However, barriers to trade become important when it comes to nontropical farm products and to manufactured and semimanufactured goods. Looking at nominal tariffs may be misleading since they are often far below effective rates of protection that are calculated relative to the value added by the industry under protection. Effective rates of protection in excess of a 100 percent can arise even in the presence of relatively low, and apparently harmless, nominal tariffs. Effective protection tends to be largest in those areas where the comparative advantages of LDCs seem the greatest. Existing tariff structures often make it uneconomical for developing nations to process their raw materials before exporting them.

Perhaps even more worrisome are nontariff barriers (NTBs). In a world where currency fluctuations can make tariffs look trivial, countries seem to rely more and more on NTBs. NTBs are particularly pernicious because they tend to be discriminatory and their real costs are difficult to measure, although they are often equivalent to prohibitive tariffs. Moreover, once in place, NTBs tend to remain for a long time; temporary measures have a remarkable propensity to become permanent. It is in everyone's interest that this trend be reversed, perhaps with the help of a multilateral agreement.

Industrialized nations will reap the benefits of freer trade. Economists have long recognized that protectionism is almost always a suboptimal policy. It is often instituted on the basis of shortsighted considerations and under the pressure of special interest groups. Fallacious thinking is commonplace in this area.

It is important to realize that the export prospects of the industrialized countries to the LDCs will be rather limited in the near future. Third World countries simply will not have the means to import anything but necessities and the equipment required for their economic development. This need not be an excessive obstacle to the development of the industrialized countries since by far the largest proportion of world trade takes place within the Organization for Economic Cooperation and Development (OECD) region. Exports to LDCs will gradually expand as the situation improves. What is the most disruptive and, hence, what should be avoided are abrupt and unexpected shifts in trade flows, such as the $8 billion drop in U.S. exports to Mexico when the bubble finally burst in 1982.

The return to prosperity and the resumption of vigorous growth in Western economies are, of course, prerequisites for any expansion of LDC exports. Sustained economic growth is only feasible in a stable and noninflationary environment. The responsibility of Western governments and central banks is to provide such a setting through sound fiscal and monetary policies.

Economic growth has picked up in a number of Western nations. It would be dangerous, however, to assume that we are about to enter an era of high and sustained growth. Too many problems remain unsolved. For example, budget deficits are larger than ever, and inflation has not been overcome either in the United States or in Europe.

Anemic economic growth in Western countries would annihilate the hopes of LDCs of expanding their exports to any significant degree, and alternative ways should be sought to reduce the debt burden of developing nations. Suggestions have been made, for instance, that debtor countries should sell some of their assets to their creditors. For those countries with large endowments of natural resources or profitable state-owned enterprises, this is certainly an option worth considering.

Such transactions would underline the willingness of debtor countries to come to grips with their problems, and they would oblige rich countries to take a more active part in the development of LDCs. Of course, schemes of this type cannot be expected to solve all problems, and they should not be allowed to cripple future prospects of LDCs. In today's situation, however, some novel thinking is badly needed, and we cannot afford to overlook any suggestions that might improve the overall picture.

The debt problem will not just go away; it will stay with us for quite some time. Austerity and growth need time to take effect. It is much the same with any economic agent trying to restructure its balance sheet. During this period it is vital that public and private financial institutions cooperate.

Private banks must play a crucial role in the restructuring effort especially since they have many billions of dollars at stake. They must offer LDCs some time. In fact, the banks need the time also since they have their own balance sheets to clean up. Patience and much discipline are necessary. We are all in the same boat, and there is no place for free riders. It may seem somewhat counterintuitive to ask banks to throw good money after bad, but there is no other way. In the present situation, the social costs of not acting far exceed the private costs. Of course, some guarantees are needed. These guarantees are provided by the austerity programs set up in cooperation with the IMF.

Time is needed because if the austerity measures are too harsh, they will not work and will not be credible. It is essential that the austerity measures be distributed fairly across social groups so that those who have benefited the least from previous excesses will not also be the ones asked now to pay most of the price. Belt tightening where it is no longer possible can only jeopardize existing political and social structures. It could lead to political and social upheaval with consequences far more dramatic than any prospect of bank failures or country defaults.

It is sometimes argued that it is in no country's interest to repudiate its foreign debt. A country that would default would have little to gain and much to lose. International trade, for one thing, would become nearly impossible, even on a barter basis. The country would end up banned from the world economy, and the resulting strangulating effect would be devastating. It seems, therefore, fair to say that no rational country will default. Unfortunately, people and governments do not always behave rationally; we are reminded of this every day.

The international financial arena is now much better prepared than in 1982 to handle a possible default as was illustrated by the speed and flexibility shown by international financial institutions and central banks in handling the Mexican emergency in 1982. We can be more confident today that the system could absorb the impact of a default. Public financial institutions could step in to avoid a domino effect. It is not a matter of bailing out private banks. Central banks are responsible for the good health of the payments system, but individual banks—and even more so, individual bankers and bank shareholders—would not necessarily escape unscarred. A succession of defaults would have some lasting real effects, and it would require some severe adjustments on the behalf of Western economies and, one might add, of OPEC creditors.

Not much has been said about low income countries, those countries where annual income per capita is less than $400 and sometimes less than $100. These countries do not have much of a debt problem because they are so poor that nobody really wants to lend to them on a commercial basis. These countries rely mostly on official development assistance through the channel of international development agencies or on a bilateral basis. Far from increasing in recent years, the flow of concessional aid has receded. But the plight of these low income countries is no less severe than that of other non-oil-exporting developing nations, and their prospects are far worse. Low income countries were badly hit by the deterioration in their terms of trade, particularly those countries that only manage to export a small number of raw materials. Demographic pressures are such that real GNP per capita is falling in many cases. Concessional assistance plays a vital role in these countries, and one can only deplore that many industrialized nations, particularly the United States, currently see fit to reduce this type of assistance. Some would say that what official channels do, private enterprise can do better and more efficiently. They point at South Korea, Singapore, or Taiwan as examples of what private initiative can achieve. They are right, of course, that private initiative can do marvels, and the recent history of these newly industrialized countries provides the best hope yet for the future, but one should not forget what triggered this spectacular growth. Indeed, most newly industrialized nations, until not so long ago, were vastly dependent on concessional aid.

Certainly the debt problem is not solved, but the danger of an uncontrollable catastrophe is considerably less than it was in 1982. Some time has been won and must now be used to set down a strategy that will pave the way for a long-term solution. That this solution cannot consist of indefinitely extending new credits to developing nations should be clear, just as the flow of money cannot be suddenly interrupted. Equally obvious is the fact that the strategy must deal with questions that extend well beyond financing matters.

The real economic adjustments required of debtors as well as creditors have already been discussed. However, there is little talk of the demographic problems that debtor countries are facing. One tends to accept them as a fact of life; often one hesitates to discuss these matters for ethical or religious reasons. However, one cannot escape this question while reflecting about ways of improving living conditions in LDCs. And, after all, this should be the ultimate purpose of our efforts.

Many debtor countries are sitting on a demographic time bomb. Population growth in Brazil and in Mexico, for instance, is in the vicinity of 2.5 percent annually. At a time when income growth has subsided as the consequence of deteriorating terms of trade and other factors, the population explosion results in a squeeze that is difficult to bear. Far from increasing, real per capita income has fallen in a number of developing countries during the last decade.

One might think that a country's population is an important national asset. Labor endowment is viewed by trade economists as a major factor of production. But a large population can also be a liability if it is mostly unskilled and in poor health and if the age distribution is skewed toward the lower end. Furthermore, if capital is scarce, the marginal product of labor could well fall below subsistence level.

A further complicating element is the rapid urbanization of LDCs as the result of population growth and rural migration. According to some projections, the population of Mexico City will reach 30 million by the year 2000, and 11 of the world's 15 largest cities will be in developing nations. Urbanization at this scale leads to massive economic, social, and political problems. Diseconomies of scale, inefficiencies, and negative externalities become widespread. Hence, the LDCs need to slow down the trend and to place more emphasis on rural development.

The crucial question is how is it possible to make the poor of these countries less poor, or expressed in economic terms, how can one get them to benefit from growth and potential welfare gains when economic growth rates that can be sustained tend to fall short of the rates of population growth? A frank and unashamed word in favor of family planning might be a more effective and more durable remedy than millions of dollars of new credits.

Part II
Economic Policies and Their International Consequences: Views from the Public Sector

2
The International Consequences of the U.S. Fiscal and Monetary Policy Mix

Anthony M. Solomon

T his chapter discusses two aspects of international monetary policy: first, the international consequences of the kind of fiscal and monetary policy mix the United States has been running and is likely to be running in the foreseeable future and second, several areas where cooperative action among the major industrial countries is possible and could be constructive, even though inevitably the United States will fall short of true harmonization of its national fiscal and monetary policies. These are related themes because the fiscal-monetary mix in the United States is a key factor in the world economy and a direct vehicle for the way it cooperates, for better or worse, with its partners abroad.

A look at the overall performance of the U.S. economy in 1983 shows a strong recovery, substantial job growth, booming profits, continued moderation in inflation (notably on the wage side), and less volatility in financial markets. In the aggregate, then, it is difficult to make the case that U.S. monetary and fiscal policies have done terrible damage up to now, at least from a domestic standpoint. From an international perspective, however, there may be somewhat more justification for complaint. It is worth recognizing at the outset that U.S. total imports grew by $46 billion between the fourth quarter 1982 and the fourth quarter 1983, and that represents about 50 percent of the growth of total world trade. The U.S. recovery has been and continues to be an engine for world expansion.

Certainly, not everyone has benefited on balance from the results of the U.S. policy mix. U.S. interest rates have been higher than they would have been if there had been a different mix of policies—for example, a smaller budget deficit and correspondingly easier monetary conditions. The high interest rates have been one of the leading reasons—but not the only reason—why the dollar has stayed extremely strong in the foreign exchange markets. U.S. exports have been a heavy casualty: export volume is down by over 25 percent from 1981. A good part of the undermining of U.S. competitiveness can be traced directly to the loose fiscal and relatively tight monetary policy mix.

A more balanced mix would have been welcomed abroad. A large number of heavily indebted nations, particularly in Latin America, would have had lower debt-servicing burdens and somewhat more manageable adjustment needs. A more balanced U.S. mix also would have made it possible for other industrialized countries to lower their interest rates more than they did. Together, these results would have promoted a faster global recovery.

This line of analysis is sensible and broadly, although not universally, accepted. Realistically, however, apart from a sweeping change in the U.S. fiscal stance, which simply would not have been possible given the positions of the administration and the majority of the Congress, and apart from a more rapid unwinding of inflation expectations than human nature seems capable of, it is hard to see how U.S. interest rates could have been drastically lower than they were during 1982 and the first half of 1983.

In the circumstances of a depressed economy, with everyone acutely sensitive to the need not to waste the progress made against inflation during a painful recession, choices were limited. Thus, the mix of a relatively stimulative fiscal policy coupled with a considerable easing in the restrictive cast of monetary policy might have been improved upon but not dramatically. The recovery would have been somewhat more balanced and interest rate burdens would have been lessened if the United States had greater fiscal discipline. Perhaps most significant, the financial markets would have been less cynical about the prospects for interest rates staying down if they had seen more evidence of a willingness to deal with fiscal deficits. Those concerns still influence market sentiment.

At the same time, a different mix would not have worked miracles. The direct impact of a smaller degree of fiscal stimulus would have tended to slow the growth of spending. Corporate profits might not have increased as fast as they have. Also, the positive effects on the rest of the world of a somewhat reduced level of U.S. interest rates would have been offset in part by a smaller increase in the U.S. trade deficit. In short, compared to the current position of the United States, there would be a different distribution of gainers and losers, but it is difficult to say how much better the outcome would be in the aggregate.

The outcome was not well foreseen by the experts. In 1982, most analysts were predicting that the unbalanced policy mix would check spending growth and lead to a weak recovery. The stimulus of larger government deficits was not fully appreciated. Too many economists focused on the level of real interest rates, which were still very high, rather than the change in rates, which was one of the steepest for any recession.

There were even some well-meaning economists who, justifiably concerned about the long-term implications of excessively large federal government deficits, fell into the trap of predicting that no recovery would be possible because of the imminent clash between a loose fiscal policy and a relatively strict monetary policy. That view was inaccurate because it misinterpreted the timing and magnitude of the effects of policy. This crying-wolf approach has unfortunately blemished what I think is the solid case that ultimately underlies the economists' legitimate concerns.

My view is that a policy mix that is basically made up of a relatively loose fiscal policy and a relatively tight monetary policy is unwise from a long-term perspective. It exposes the economy to a greater risk of cyclical instability. It will tend to retard capital investment, and eventually U.S. growth potential will be lower. It threatens to make financial markets more unstable and has a broader political cost as well. It casts doubt on whether U.S. institutions and system of representative government are capable of resolving competing claims on resources. It tells the world that the American people want more goods and services from their government than they are willing to pay for. That is not a good long-term message to be giving.

My judgment is that the United States would have been wiser to have made a start at the longer-term budget problem in 1982 or earlier. But it did not. Thus, until some meaningful action is taken by the Congress and the administration on expenditure levels, taxes, or both, the United States will have to look ahead to a more or less permanent condition of high budget deficits relative to national income and savings. Correspondingly, over time, monetary policy will have to tilt toward restraint if the public is going to have confidence that inflation will not revive.

Unfortunately, that mix yields built-in vulnerabilities. It requires exacting fine tuning by the Federal Reserve to prevent inflationary impulses from reverberating through the economy. That is because historically, even where there has been the will to modify fiscal policy to assist in an anti-inflation effort, it has proved simply too cumbersome to change quickly. There is no reason to believe that it will be any easier in the future. Therefore, with monetary policy forced to carry the heavier anti-inflation burden over any short-term time horizon, and with deregulation of the financial system now far advanced, substantial increases in interest rates may have to occur from time to time before demand pressures are checked and inflation slows. However, those increases would be on top of what are already high rates. The financial implications of that threat leave the U.S. economy potentially more unstable than would be the case under a more orthodox policy mix.

The vulnerability to financial stress is magnified when we look at the international consequences of this longer-term mismatch in policies. First, the foreign currency markets may be very likely to produce repeated wide swings in exchange rates, and from the perspective of world trade there will probably be a lot of overshooting. This occurrence would give many distorted signals about relative competitiveness and would aggravate tensions in the trade area. Second, because of the nature of the outstanding debt of the major LDCs with severe debt-servicing problems—heavily dollar denominated and on a floating rate basis—the chances of the LDCs' making full adjustment to their recent economic crisis will be less good. There may well be a greater danger of one or more countries' being simply unable to bear the debt burden in full. Finally, the other industrialized countries may grow tired of being whipsawed by interest rate and exchange rate fluctuations that they view as originating in the United States. They might seek ways to insulate themselves behind various kinds of trade, exchange control, or capital control barriers.

While this list of unfortunate outcomes is not a certainty, it repre sents a risk that can be avoided or at least substantially reduced by taking action to deal with the source of the danger—namely, the large future federal budget deficits. That makes sense from a domestic point of view because it means that there will be more scope for growth in interest-rate-sensitive sectors such as housing, business fixed investment, and exports. Thus, it will have a long-term payoff in terms of higher productivity. Smaller budget deficits make sense from an international point of view because they improve the chances of achieving the sustained growth in the world economy and trade necessary for resolving serious debt problems and preserving an open world trading system. I hope economists can get this message across to those in Washington with the power to do something about the fiscal deficit before they are forced to do something with the sorts of adverse outcomes I have described.

The first best policy is to change the mix by getting the kinds of difficult ideological and political compromises that would be required. But we have to realize that even with the first best solution there will be delays, possibly long delays, between action and the ultimate positive effects on the economy and on the financial markets. We have to recognize that, to varying degrees, the policy mixes that have been followed by other major countries have not been perfect either. The world's economic problems are not caused by the imperfections in U.S. policies alone.

Thus, even in the best case the United States will be confronted with the problems of exchange rate volatility, LDC debt-servicing difficulties, and pressures for protectionism—at least for a transitional period. Consequently, it is worth doing some serious thinking about steps that can be taken to mitigate the international consequences of less than perfect mixes of policies on the part of the United States and other major countries.

On the dollar question, a majority of people involved in industry and the exchange markets feel that the dollar is certainly very high at current levels in terms of our export competitiveness. An even larger majority feel that a further rise in the dollar would qualify as overshooting in these terms. Many of the same people acknowledge that the possibility exists that later on the very large current account deficits could induce a major shift in market conditions and a disorderly fall of the dollar.

An extreme move in either direction could prove very damaging to the U.S. economy. A further rise in the dollar would have a punishing effect on remaining exports and on domestic industries trying to compete with cheap imports. A rapid and disorderly fall in the dollar, by contrast, could inject a source of price pressure into the U.S. economy at the worst time: When U.S. expansion is reaching maturity, the amount of spare capacity left to reemploy is nearly exhausted, and the potential for inflationary effects is the greatest.

No one can say with any perfect certainty what the appropriate level of exchange rates should be. But there must be a point where a more hands-on approach by the authorities of the principal industrial countries, acting in concert, toward developments in the exchange markets can be a useful adjunct in helping to maintain orderly conditions while other more fundamental adjustments are under way.

On the LDC debt-servicing problem, the United States should be asking what can be done, during a period of difficult economic adjustments, to shore up the ability of borrowers to meet their obligations. This is an area where a large measure of international cooperation is essential not just among governments and central banks but also with commercial bank lenders.

No one prescription will be sufficient, and many ideas must be considered. For instance, one approach that may be constructive in certain cases would be to reduce the spreads on reschedulings to levels more in accord with the debtor countries' near-term ability to repay. Some steps that are being taken in this direction are worth watching closely.

Beyond these suggestions, the United States must work to reduce the interest rate and exchange rate risks that many of the LDCs will inevitably face in the period ahead. This basic principle is important: Debt reschedulings should leave borrowers who are pursuing reasonable adjustment programs in a strengthened position both to meet the renegotitiated terms and to absorb unforeseen shocks including unanticipated increases in market interest rates.

Finally, on the trade issue, I believe that the most effective way of staving off protectionist pressures is to initiate a multilateral round of negotiations for further trade liberalization. As some observers would say, a good offense is the best defense. Without major initiatives, the temptations for a piecemeal chipping away at liberal trading principles are enormous. Therefore, the time has come for the Reagan round. The items on the agenda are well recognized. They include developing an effective safeguards code, as well as dealing with trade in services, high technology, information, and agriculture. The agenda has to encompass the issues of major importance to heavily indebted developing countries. If there were any doubts about the need to move in this direction before, they have to have been swept away by the absolute necessity of preserving the access of troubled LDC debtor countries to industrialized country markets as well as to each other's markets. Realistically, trade liberalization has to happen on terms that are broadly perceived as being fair and in a multilateral context.

In summary, my basic critique of the unfortunate long-term fiscal-monetary policy mix that is now in store for the United States is that it is risky. Yes, with a considerable amount of monetary fine tuning, only a few external shocks, and good luck, sustainable growth with low inflation could be achieved under that mix. However, that is asking a lot. Many of the risks are borne not only by the United States and its citizens but also by the rest of the world. The present combination of U.S. economic policies increases the risks of financial stress, paves the way for a period of extended volatility in the exchange markets, and opens wider the door for protectionist actions on behalf of special interests. These threats can be curtailed by timely actions to achieve a better balance of fiscal and monetary policies; but time is running short, and deliberate action is needed before it runs out.

3
An Assessment of Macroeconomic Policy: A Japanese Perspective

Shijuro Ogata

This chapter assesses the achievements (and failures) of macroeconomic policies, particularly fiscal and monetary policies, in the leading industrialized countries during 1983. After the second oil crisis, the extremely difficult problems included, inter alia, violent inflation, stagnation of economic growth, a large balance of payments disequilibrium, extremely high interest rates, exchange rate instability, widespread protectionism, and international debt problems. Even though there were some improvements during the latter part of 1983, many unsettled issues remain, and the following sections examine them separately.

Inflation

There have been substantial improvements in the performance of prices in the major industrialized countries. Not only has the rate of inflation been reduced, but also differential rates of inflation between different countries have narrowed. This reduction is, in most cases, due to the restrictive monetary policies adopted in those countries that have more than offset the adverse impact of undisciplined easy fiscal policies. In addition, a greater flexibility in wage settlements, which have been gradually influenced by the demand and supply conditions of labor markets in a number of countries, contributed to the deceleration of inflation.

However, one cannot be complacent about inflation. In many places inflationary expectations remain for a variety of reasons. For example, the large fiscal deficits in many countries tend to give rise to an understandable apprehension of the danger of the monetarization of fiscal deficits through excessive monetary expansion. It is not impossible, either, that the painful debt burden of public and private borrowers might make them rather nostalgic for settling their debts through inflation.

Stagnation of Economic Growth

In 1982 the economic recovery started in the United States and in some other major countries. This recovery is generally due to the deceleration of inflation and the subsequent revival of consumer confidence. In the case of the United States where the recovery has been stronger and more broadly based than originally expected, one cannot deny the role of policy stimuli such as tax deductibility of interest payments and the greater depreciation allowances for business corporations, which have enabled both housing investment and corporate activities to recover despite the continuation of high real interest rates. It is also true to some extent that the stronger dollar and the subsequent deterioration of the competitiveness of U.S. industries have helped the export-led recovery of other countries.

However, it is not clear whether or not the recovery in other major industrial countries is solidly established. Recovery in the United States has been broadly based. Some countries are far behind. Other countries are taking advantage of the U.S. economic recovery. In some countries domestic demand is not strong. Even where domestic recovery is strong, often it is based mainly on inventory cycles and consumer demand and is not supported by private investment. In any event, the employment situation has not improved satisfactorily.

Balance of Payments Disequilibrium

Improvement in the balance of payments has been remarkable. The surpluses of the oil-producing countries have been substantially reduced, while the efforts for balance of payments adjustment of some of the debtor countries have produced favorable results. Oil-consuming countries, developed as well as developing, are gradually improving their balance of payments situations.

Nevertheless, not only do the deficits of non-oil-producing developing countries remain substantial, but also a new imbalance has emerged and is growing. The United States is running a large deficit while Japan is running a large surplus not only vis-à-vis the entire world but also with each other. In the case of the United States, the combination of a strong dollar and a strong domestic recovery has resulted in a large current account deficit. In the case of Japan, the sharp reduction of oil imports, the growth of exports, and the slow recovery of domestic demand are responsible for the large surplus.

Interest Rates

Since summer 1982, interest rates in the United States and a number of other major countries have declined, in certain cases, from two-digit rates to single-digit rates in the short end. Interest rates in the major industrialized countries have tended to converge. Such developments are probably due to deceleration of inflation, slower growth of the money supply, and to some extent, slower economic growth itself.

However, if you compare present nominal rates of interest with the present rates of inflation, real interest rates are still unusually high. This may be partly attributable to the existence of rather high inflationary expectations despite the fact that the current rate of inflation happens to be fairly low.

Though some prominent people in the United States may disagree, I think that the continuation of large fiscal deficits in most of the major countries is one factor behind the continuing high interest rates. There is a clear gap between the equilibrium rates of interest in the United States and those in other countries, where equilibrium rates of interest are defined as interest rates compatible with economic recovery.

This gap is probably due to greater tax deductibility that exists mainly in the United States. The unusually high real interest rates may not be so harmful to the U.S. economy, but they are definitely painful for other countries, particularly debtor countries.

Exchange Rates

During the last part of 1983, exchange rate volatility was substantially reduced. The range of fluctuation of the dollar rate against other major currencies was narrower in 1983 than in 1982. This reduced volatility is attributable to converging economic performances of the major industrialized countries, particularly a convergence of the rates of inflation as well as rates of interest.

The moderate rate of growth as well as small fluctuations in the U.S. money supply may have reduced the excessive monetaristic reaction of the financial and exchange markets. Occasional intervention by the monetary authorities of major industrial countries has also helped to reduce exchange rate volatility.

However, exchange rates of major currencies must be considered as misaligned when compared with the fundamental conditions of the economies of major currency countries. It is not easy to judge whether the current exchange rates of certain currencies are overvalued or undervalued, but we still tend to compare the exchange rates of currencies with the relative price performance and the relative current account development.

Because of the growing magnitude of capital flows and the greater sensitivity of the general public to international developments, exchange rates are more influenced by interest rate differentials, capital movements, and political factors. Although it can be argued that exchange rates do reflect the point of equilibrium between demand and supply in the exchange market, the present levels of exchange rates tend to disappoint those who expect that the exchange rates should reflect the relative price or current account performance and should function to help adjustment in current account imbalances.

Protectionism

In the area of protectionism, improvements are few and not remarkable. There is a growing recognition of the danger of protectionism in official as well as private circles, and a number of discussions have begun in various forms about the importance of a relationship between macroeconomic policies and trade policies. It is definitely a good step forward to recognize the impact of macroeconomic policies such as fiscal and monetary policies on protectionist forces. Nevertheless, despite repeated outright denunciations of protectionism by reasonable and responsible people, protectionism not only exists but also persists. The continuation of a high level of unemployment in many countries, despite the beginning of economic recovery; the existence of structural pessimism in some countries where structural adjustment has been delayed; and the misalignment of exchange rates or the perception of misalignment of exchange rates are factors responsible for the spread of protectionism.

Although Japanese protectionism exists, particularly with regard to agricultural products, about 40 percent of Japanese exports to the United States and about 15 or 20 percent of the Japanese exports to the entire world are at present subject to the so-called voluntary but actually involuntary restraint program, a disguised form of trade protectionism. This is only one of many examples of protectionist practices.

International Debt Problems

In spite of continuing concern, there have been clear improvements in international debt problems. Adjustment policies of some of the debtor countries, like Mexico, have been carried out despite much political and social pain. The economic recovery of major industrialized countries is helping the debtor countries' adjustments. Unlike the summer of 1982, a procedure has been gradually established to cope with debt problems. Debtor countries are showing a greater willingness than before to consult with the IMF and other international financial institutions. The timely formation of advisory committees by leading lending banks and the coordinated support of monetary authorities of creditor countries are positive developments. Even then, a number of difficult problems lie ahead. Not all adjustments in debtor countries have been successful because of political and social factors. In view of the fiscal constraints in major industrialized countries and the magnitude of bank lending already extended, it is not easy to secure a stable flow of capital to the developing countries. Despite the recovery of major industrial economies, high interest rates in international markets continue to be a great burden on debtor countries. Protectionism also is detrimental to the recovery of the economies of debtor countries.

Having reviewed improvements and remaining difficulties on seven major fronts, it must be emphasized that the leading developed countries now face the need to sustain noninflationary growth they hope with lower interest rates and with a stronger resistance to protectionism, not only for themselves but also for the benefit of the world as a whole.

In the area of fiscal policy there is an urgent need to reduce fiscal deficits to give more room for private business activities and investment and to allow greater flexibility in fiscal policy itself. Since the structural aspects of deficits cannot be corrected overnight, those countries that find themselves in a stronger economic position might better intensify their efforts as soon as possible to reduce their deficits while still taking advantage of economic upswings.

However, in a number of other countries the recovery is not strong, and, therefore, the need to remain flexible continues so these countries can cope with cyclical problems. Fiscal policy is by nature not easily reversible in practice. It is difficult to determine how those countries can or should deviate from the medium-term objective of reestablishing fiscal discipline, particularly when there is a lack of strong political leadership.

With respect to monetary policy, economists agree about the importance of reestablishing and maintaining the credibility of the monetary authorities' determination to fight against inflation. In practice, however, it is not always clear how to maintain such credibility, whether faithfully sticking to the previously established formulas and targets or by being more flexible in deviating from the predetermined targets, given the circumstances. Thus, there is a choice between credibility by persistence and credibility by flexibility. Probably both are important, depending upon the situation.

The importance of exchange rate implications for monetary policy in the leading developed countries must be emphasized. Now that exchange rates are strongly influenced by relative monetary conditions in the major industrialized countries, a careful consideration of exchange rate movements is required for the conduct of monetary policy. Also, the usefulness of timely exchange market intervention through central bank cooperation should not be disregarded.

Following are some observations about Japanese economic policy. In Japan domestic prices are very stable. With an annual rate of increase in consumer prices of 1.4 percent, it is safe to say that inflationary expectations are almost nil. The economy is expected to grow at a rate of 3.5 percent in FY 1983 and at 4 percent by FY 1985.

However, there are a number of difficult problems. First, domestic demand is not strong enough. Its contribution to real growth during the first half of 1983 was less than a half. Second, the current account surplus in 1983 exceeded $20 billion, and more of the same is expected for 1984. Third, the exchange rate of the Japanese yen against the U.S. dollar is still considered by many observers to be undervalued. Fourth, the combination of the vast current account surplus and undervalued exchange rate is giving rise to spreading protectionism, as I have already touched upon. Under such circumstances, Japan needs to strengthen domestic demand, to reduce or at least prevent a further increase in the current account surplus, and to strengthen the Japanese yen.

Despite many constraints already referred to, Japan announced in October 1983 a number of fiscal and monetary measures including increased public expenditure, tax reductions, and a modest reduction in the discount rate. These measures may not be able to produce quick results, but they are steps in the right direction.

Finally, I present two additional points. First, price stability will continue to be the basis of sustainable economic growth. Japanese policymakers are determined not to repeat mistakes made during the early 1970s when the need to overcome domestic stagnation and current account surpluses was overemphasized. The result was an excessive growth of the monetary supply and violent inflation, which contributed to worldwide inflation, eventually leading to the first oil crisis.

Second, more than any time before, policymakers in Japan are conscious of the international implications of their national economic policies. If and when the U.S. dollar peaks, as has been predicted for some time, those in charge of Japanese monetary policy will be most careful in keeping a good balance between two policy objectives: one, the strengthening of the yen, and the other, the strengthening of the domestic economy, two objectives that do not always go hand in hand.

4

The World Economic Crisis and Export Financing

William H. Draper III

The Export-Import Bank (Eximbank) of the United States is the only government agency that is directly given the task of supporting sales of U.S. goods and services to buyers in other countries. It supplements and encourages private sector financing to fill certain gaps left by commercial banks, and it compensates for many private market imperfections caused by foreign government interference. Eximbank extends direct loans and guarantees and insures repayment of loans made by others. The purpose of the bank has remained the same since it was founded almost 50 years ago. The emphasis has not changed during most of the period, but occasionally Eximbank has had to respond to changing needs.

The bank was started in 1934 to prime the pump with exports during the Depression. It helped to keep trade lanes open during World War II, including loans to build the Burma Road. It helped U.S. firms participate in the postwar reconstruction of Europe and Asia prior to the Marshall Plan. In the 1950s it helped U.S. firms to tap growing developing countries' markets.

Huge projects were begun in the 1960s. The large jet aircraft and nuclear power projects of that time became fashionable in almost every country that had a sizable population. The amount of money required and the extended repayment periods often exceeded commercial bank capabilities, requiring participation of Eximbank. Of course, the commercial bankers continued to participate in ever increasing amounts all through those years, and the bank was granting only those loans and guarantees that commercial banks could not or would not grant.

The 1970s were marked by expansive borrowing, soaring commercial interest rates, and intense competition. Much of that competition was among governments trying to subsidize the financing of many large projects. The 1970s opened with a sudden and unexpected change in the world economy. Since 1979, the price of oil has tripled. The real exchange value of the dollar rose 55 percent. Real interest rates reached unprecedented heights. Leading industrial nations were thrown into a prolonged recession. Commercial banks lost confidence in international lending as increasing numbers of foreign borrowers experienced difficulties in repaying their debts.

Resource-rich developing countries were especially hard hit by these economic changes. There was an increasing percentage of floating rate loans to be repaid at unanticipated high rates. These countries had a loss of sales of their exports to recession-hit industrial nations. The poorer developing countries' commodity prices hit a 30-year low.

Argentina, Brazil, and Mexico accounted for 30 percent of all developing countries' debts in 1981. These three countries represented 36 percent of all debt servicing in the developing countries, while from 1978 to 1981, their interest payments rose 170 percent, from $6 billion to $16.2 billion.

During 1982, the whole international financial community has been shaken by the debt repayment crises in major high growth nations. International financing flows declined. Medium-term international bank credit commitments fell 32 percent from $145 billion in 1981 to $98 billion in 1982, further compounding the developing countries' problems.

In the first half of 1983, the BIS reported that, for the first time in 20 years, second-quarter figures showed only very marginal growth in international bank activity. Commercial banks' gross external assets were up less than 0.5 percent, and they actually declined in real terms.

International bank lending was one-half of what it had been in the second quarter of 1982. New lending to Latin American countries dropped from $2.7 billion to $1 billion. The financial crisis dealt a body blow to exports, and the improvement of U.S. exports is Eximbank's responsibility. World exports fell 1.8 percent from 1980 to 1981 and fell a further 7 percent between 1981 and 1982. U.S. exports, which had grown every year since the late 1950s, dropped 9.2 percent in 1982 and dropped a further 10.4 percent in the first half of 1983.

U.S. exports to non-oil-exporting African nations fell 16.7 percent in 1982 and were down a further 20 percent in the first half of 1983. U.S. exports to non-oil-exporting Latin American countries were down 22 percent in 1982 and down an additional 32.4 percent in the first half of 1983. The reported U.S. trade deficit in October 1983 alone was $9 billion. It will probably be $100 billion in 1984.

The crisis has had a fourfold effect on Eximbank. First, as U.S. exports dropped, so did demand for Eximbank's financing services. In 1981, the bank authorized $12.9 billion in loans, guarantees, and insurance support for U.S. exports. For FY 1982 and again for FY 1983, the bank's authorizations were $9.3 billion, down 27 percent for the FY 1981 level.

Second, there has been a shift in the mix of Eximbank's program support during the past 3 years. The number of large projects and major capital equipment export sales requiring the bank's long-term direct loans has fallen dramatically. Foreign governments are putting these big projects off to an ever receding horizon and in some cases properly so. At the same time, as commercial lenders became more and more concerned with the risks of international transactions, the call for Eximbank's guarantee and insurance supports remained strong.

In 1981, Eximbank's loans represented 42 percent of its authorizations. Guarantees and insurance were 58 percent. In 1982, the loans were 38 percent and guarantees were 62 percent, and in 1983, loans accounted for only 9 percent and guarantees and insurance 91 percent.

Part of the reason for the change is because Eximbank has negotiated with the OECD, an arrangement that has put bank interest rates at a level comparable to commercial rates. The bank is trying to eliminate subsidies in accordance with both President Reagan's program and the desires of the other OECD countries. The problem is that everybody thinks that if they do not subsidize, they will lose exports. In truth, the biggest subsidizers, France and the United Kingdom, are the only countries that lost market shares in the last 3 years.

Third, the dramatic changes in the international economy affected the bank's portfolio of previously approved transactions. The bank has had a spate of claims and reschedulings. It has had to assign two special task forces to help work through a record number of claims received under its guarantee and insurance programs.

The bank's record of recovering claims is excellent. It has reached an agreement in principle with the government of Mexico regarding private sector claims that followed the Mexican crisis. Eximbank has recently recovered $419 million outstanding from Iran. The Iranian settlement brought Eximbank's total delinquencies from about the $800 million level to about $400 million. There are still several hundred million dollars of debt in Poland that may take a while to collect, and claims are piling up in Venezuela, which worries Eximbank.

With regard to rescheduling, the bank has rescheduled principal and interest installments on its loans for some borrowers who are encountering temporary difficulties. One reason for this move was to aid collectibility, and another reason was to enable the obligor to service the debt. As a major international lender, the bank participated in seventeen Paris Club countrywide debt reschedulings between January 1981 and August 1983.

Fourth, Eximbank is undertaking a careful analysis of its loans to fulfill its congressional mandate for finding reasonable assurance of repayment in these hectic days. The bank's programs remain active and the economists who are advising it on whether or not there is reasonable assurance for repayment feel a bit like a rubber band that is being stretched nearly to the breaking point. Past efforts were largely directed toward assessing the creditworthiness of the individual purchaser and the ability of the individual project to generate sufficient income to repay debt undertaken for its development.

In today's world, however, country analysis has assumed a new importance. Eximbank takes a long-range view. It considers that resource-rich countries have long-term creditworthiness as long as they are taking measures to correct their temporary debt-servicing problems. Eximbank is taking a leadership role in keeping the flow of credits moving to countries with temporary liquidity problems.

First, it takes the view of a venture capitalist. With a problem company, it sometimes takes more money to get out than to get in. But it often is worth staying in, and Eximbank believes it will be worth it in the case of Brazil, Mexico, and many of the other resource-rich countries with debt problems. However, achieving liquidity takes time. Eximbank agrees with the commercial bankers that they are confronting problems of liquidity and not insolvency.

For some temporary financing solutions, Eximbank can act as a catalyst in putting together international rescue efforts. For example, the $1.5 billion guarantee program that was approved for Brazil in September 1982 led to an $11 billion international safety net. However, in order to put in that $1.5 billion, the bank insisted that the commercial banks put in an additional $6.5 billion of fresh money. It also insisted that the Brazilians be in complete compliance with the IMF and that if they are not, Eximbank's $1.5 billion export credit facility will be removed. Thus, all participants have got to work together.

Eximbank played a similar role in 1982 when it participated in the $10 billion safety net that Mexico required. I was impressed at the IMF meetings in Toronto when international bankers and government officials worked together to come to a practical solution.

Mexico is taking the appropriate corrective measures. However, doubling the price of gasoline, food and electricity, is difficult politically. Cutting a third of the purchasing power from the middle income people is really a difficult political problem.

Finally, Eximbank is meeting increasing Latin American and African demands from commercial banks for Eximbank and FCIA short-term insurance coverage for credit sales of bulk agricultural and industrial raw materials and spare parts exports. This has become essential in some countries just to keep the grist running through the mill, allowing the mills to operate.

The international financial system has been tested as never before and is making the necessary adjustments to meet the challenge. Member contributions to the IMF and other key international organizations are increasing. IMF-structured programs are helping many nations to plan and implement reforms that will solve their problems. Programs are now under way and should restore the credit rating of Brazil and Mexico by 1986 or 1987.

Imports have been cut back as far as they can be without further damaging economies and jeopardizing recovery. Exports of developing nations must be increased to generate the foreign exchange needed to service debt and to rebuild. Government lenders like Eximbank are providing essential assistance through new credits, rescheduling, and special insurance plans to facilitate commercial financing. Commercial banks are playing a key role in cooperation with government and international lenders.

In conclusion, only through a truly cooperative effort will international financial institutions succeed in restoring real growth to the international economy. All are in this together. When the developing countries solve their problems, they will once again be a growing market for the products and services of the industrialized countries as well as being centers of profitable new business for bankers. Industrialized nations must keep their markets open to imports from the developing nations so they can build up their foreign exchange reserves. Eximbank is proud of its part in the process of rebuilding the international economic order. It has altered its emphasis many times over the past 50 years to provide assistance to U.S. exporters. It has risen to meet today's special challenges of tomorrow.

Part III
Changing Financial Markets and International Economic Policies: Views from the Private Sector

5
Money Markets: New Pressures and Movements

Scott E. Pardee

I n spring 1983, Chairman Volcker of the Federal Reserve addressed the American Forex Club, the association of foreign exchange traders. At the time, the odds seemed heavily against Volcker's being reappointed even though it was widely recognized that he had done a good job. Foreign exchange traders are a self-assured lot, and they have a particularly cynical attitude toward government officials. Nevertheless, that evening they gave Volcker a hero's welcome, with a standing ovation at the outset, warm applause throughout, and another standing ovation at the end. His speech was good, as usual, and closed with one of his few efforts at waxing philosophic if not actually poetic. The thought he expressed was that if inflation could be brought under control here and abroad and if interest rate differentials narrowed, the exchange markets would be much more orderly. Volcker then said, "The aim is not to deprive you of your joy or your livelihood. Rather, we want to provide you with long and lazy afternoons of placid trading."

This piece of imagery was well received since it came at a time when exchange rate movements had been exceedingly erratic, causing losses even to seasoned dealers. Afterward, however, some of the traders said that on second thought the comment scared them. Long and lazy afternoons of placid trading are afternoons in which it is difficult to make money. Traders prefer markets that have a certain amount of rate volatility, especially volatility that they can predict. The central banker's dream of a perfect market and the trader's ideal of a perfect market are not the same. The trader's ideal afternoon would be as follows: The trader goes long on a currency; the currency rises; he makes some good trades and builds his position further; the currency rises further; and at the close he finally covers in at a substantial profit. He goes home that evening square and has a long and lazy night of placid sleeping.

My observations are from the perspective of the trader, looking both at the U.S. economy and U.S. interest rates and at the international economy and foreign exchange rates. It is easy to paint a very positive picture of the U.S. economy. The expansion seems to be continuing strongly, with an annual growth rate of almost 5 percent in the fourth quarter of 1983. Retail sales seemed to hesitate briefly in November, but the Christmas season saw very strong demand, not only for the novelty items like Cabbage Patch Kids dolls but also for upscale products such as VCRs and home computers. Automobile sales and housing seem to be losing some of their steam, but capital goods expenditures are picking up. The foreign sector continues to lag, but the intensity of the pain does not seem to be as great as before. Most analysts expect some moderation of the pace of the expansion in 1984. No one sees a serious chance of recession until 1985 at the earliest.

Many things are still wrong, however. The massive U.S. fiscal deficits have been very damaging. The debate in Washington is incredible. Anyone who thinks that the deficits do not matter should sit in the trading room of a primary dealer of U.S. government securities while bidding is going on for an auction. The dealer's effort is to place the securities with investors, the customers. But investors have been repeatedly burned by buying Treasuries and then watching them decline in price shortly afterward. There is an old adage on Wall Street that it is hard to sell a bond to a man who smokes a pipe. It is even harder to sell a bond to a man when the last bond you sold him is underwater. On several occasions this year, investors were asked to bid on new Treasuries when all of the issues in the previous quarterly cycle of auctions were trading below par.

Consequently, investors require a substantial concession in interest rates before they look at any issue seriously. Dealers bidding for their own account have also been increasingly cautious—bidding higher rates to protect themselves should the market back up after they buy the securities and before the securities can be distributed. There are so many Treasury auctions and each auction is so large that the market does not have an opportunity to recover from the pressure of individual auctions. The effect is like repeated blows of a sledgehammer on the market; at times it seems like a jackhammer. While this is elementary, it seems to have been forgotten in much of the debate in Washington over the effects of the deficit. With deficits this large, taking up the lion's share of national savings, the Treasury is in effect crowding itself out.

Up to now, corporate demands for credit have been rather passive, outside of continuing efforts to extend maturities on previous debt and otherwise to improve corporate balance sheets. Many companies have had sufficient cash flow to finance their needs internally for inventories and for small investment projects. Traders carefully watch the weekly numbers on commercial and industrial loans and commercial paper, which have begun rising modestly recently, as an early indicator of when the collision will occur between the borrowing requirements of the U.S. Treasury and private credit demand. Many analysts expect that the combined force of these demands on the market will push up interest rates directly. Should the Fed try to hold rates down by providing added liquidity, traders believe that rates might stay down at first but would rise later on a resurgence in inflationary expectations.

Many economists who follow the U.S. deficit closely are scaling down their estimates for FY 1984. Economists at Discount Corporation of New York are expecting $165 billion, but other estimates are lower and the best anyone can see is $125 billion. In FY 1983 the deficit was $195 billion. The improvement largely reflects the pickup in revenues as a result of the economic expansion. No one, however, really challenges the idea that we are faced with a structural deficit of at least $100 billion, which will probably grow over the years ahead to $200 billion or worse unless something drastic is done to curb it.

The feeling among market people—traders, investors, and economists—is that the United States is being poorly served by its political leaders in the administration and Congress for not dealing seriously with the deficit now. There is a lot of posturing back and forth, but most market participants are convinced that nothing will be done until after the election, if then. If our political leaders prove us wrong and come up with a formula for reducing the structural deficit by $50 or $100 billion beginning in 1985, there could be a rally in the market that would take one's breath away. Otherwise, the jackhammer effects of Treasury auctions on the markets will continue.

Meanwhile, the markets are fearful that the recent trend of events in the Middle East, in Central America and the Carribbean, and even in Western Europe could lead to a considerable increase in military expenditures, swelling the deficit even further. Market participants spend hours swapping frightening scenarios of wars and financial collapse and discussing what they should do to protect themselves in each possible case. Ironically, U.S. Treasury securities, because they are in excess supply, always rank high as a safe refuge, if not the safest. Not only is it because of the perceived lack of credit risk since they are backed by the full faith and credit of the U.S. government but also because people feel that if war breaks out interest rates would be pushed down by fiat, as in World War II, and the only market with any liquidity left would be for Treasuries. I do not want to be alarmist, but many serious-minded people are scared, and it affects their behavior in markets.

The inflation rate is still very much better than it was, but inflation is certainly not considered dead. To be sure, some traders and economists argue that the United States is in a deflationary phase of a longer economic cycle, pointing to the high real interest rates we have had since 1979 and to the recent weakness in the gold price. Even so, many market people have taken note of the fact that the consumer price index (CPI), which rose by some 3 percent in 1982, has risen by an annual average of nearly 5 percent in 1983. Moreover, one of the key outcomes in the scenario-swapping sessions is a growing belief on the part of traders that much higher rates of inflation are inevitable. People are prepared to jump at the earliest sign of a revival of inflation in the United States. There is a great deal of disagreement over which commodity traders should jump to—gold, oil stocks, real estate—but they will not wait. I agree fully with Volcker and others at the Fed who have argued that the United States should not be complacent about a 5 percent rate of inflation. The problem with inflation is that there is no equilibrium rate. The faster prices rise, the more people expect them to rise further. The United States needs to strive for a further reduction in the inflation rate; zero is the only viable goal.

In general, the Federal Reserve has a great deal of credibility in the market. The central bank has had to shoulder the bulk of the burden of fighting inflation and since 1979 has taken an approach, brutal as it may be, that has had positive results. On a day-to-day, week-to-week basis, however, the market is very nervous over what the Federal Reserve is doing. At this time, the Federal Reserve is being unusually uncommunicative about its short-term objectives.

Recent releases of the decisions of the open market committee note that in formulating policy, the Federal Reserve considers the real economy, the inflation rate, and domestic and international financial conditions. Taking into account how these factors are behaving, the Fed looks at the monetary aggregates. I have no quarrel with the items on that list and even applaud the order of priorities it implies. In the past, the Federal Reserve tended to ignore international considerations while, to me, it gave too much attention to the monetary aggregates.

M1 in particular has been downgraded so that its growth rate is plotted in a so-called monitoring range. I think this was wise, given the erratic behavior of M1 over time. Even so, the market has not downgraded M1 as an indicator. The M1 number influences money market trading all week prior to its release each Friday. Beginning on Monday, money market economists put together their surveys and estimates of what the number will be that Friday. Despite this, for all the talent and energy that go into forecasting the M1 number, there have been occasions in which every single one of the Fed watchers has been wrong, not only in the amount of M1 growth but also in its direction. A surprise number can have a devastating effect on market psychology, on interest rates, and on exchange rates. The effect of an individual surprise number may not last very long, but the combined effects of surprises over time have added to the state of uncertainty in the market.

The Federal Reserve's communication problem—and I think it is serious—is how to indicate to the market when policy is being tightened, eased, or left essentially unchanged. When Federal Reserve officials talk about policy, they use general terminology and verbs that express degrees of change but not with precision. Seldom does anyone in the Fed say policy has tightened or eased; rather, they have become more or less accommodative. To the Fed, a tightening or an easing is something major, something that would move interest rates by a 1/2 to 1 percentage point or more. To the market, any rise in the federal funds rate is considered a tightening, and any decline in the rate is an easing. Federal Reserve officials have other terminology for smaller moves, such as a *snugging up* or a *shading* of policy, and at times they even use the term *nuance*.

I was once trying to explain the distinctions in these terms to an experienced French money market dealer. I suggested that if the Fed acted to raise the funds rate from its current level of 9 1/4 percent to 9 3/4 or 10 percent, that would be considered a tightening. If it acted to raise the rate from 9 1/4 percent to 9 1/2 percent, that would be described as a snugging up. If, however, it raised the rate from 9 1/4 to 9 3/8, that would be described as a nuance. My friend responded by saying, "Mon cher ami, that is not a nuance, that is an eighth."

The market not only looks at the federal funds rate as an indicator of current Federal Reserve policy but also watches the net reserve position of the banks, whether there are net borrowed or net free reserves, as an indicator of the relative tightness or ease of credit conditions. If the federal funds rate moves up from 9 1/4 to 9 1/2, and if net borrowed reserves increase from $100 million to $250 million, this will be considered a tightening of policy, no matter what the Federal Reserve calls it. Since this is such a small move and may quickly be washed out in subsequent weeks' figures, Federal Reserve officers are not likely to comment, which leaves the market guessing.

As I noted at the outset, traders try to position themselves ahead of rate moments. If they are initially correct, they are inclined to build on the initial position to profit from a trend. Consequently, each time the funds rate drops from, say, 9 3/8 to 9 1/8 and net borrowed reserves decline, or indeed the net reserve figure swings through zero and into free reserves, some traders begin to go long in the market. They hope that this is the beginning of a larger move by the Fed, with the funds rate perhaps breaking below 9 percent, possibly to 8 3/4 or lower. Even the initial move tends to affect the markets for fixed income securities, equities, and foreign exchange. The newspapers are quickly filled with conjecture that the Fed is easing. Then, when in fact the federal funds rate rises again and the net borrowed reserve position also increases, the whole process is reversed, causing losses to those who were late to join the Fed-is-easing bandwagon and late to leave it. With the funds rate up, the newspapers are then filled with conjecture that the Fed is tightening. Since late summer 1983, this tilting back and forth has occurred several times. In all likelihood except for a slight easing in September, the Fed has maintained a steady policy, using wider parameters for movements in both the federal funds rate and the net borrowed reserves.

In the atmosphere that exists today of fear, uncertainty, and lack of hard information on what the authorities are doing, a number of important developments are worth pointing out. First, the yield curve is incredibly steep, with short Treasury bills trading below 9 percent and the long bonds trading at nearly 12 percent. Investors are reluctant to extend out the curve in an environment in which the Fed may be tightening, the Treasury may be strapping another $150 billion or so of securities on investors next year, and a nuclear holocaust could take place because of some colossal miscalculation in Moscow and Washington.

Second, there is a greater interest than ever in options on stocks, bonds, and even foreign currencies. Why risk large losses by buying a security or a currency and having it suddenly go down sharply in price when you can instead buy a call option that can still give you a profit if you are right while it limits your potential loss if you are wrong? Options are a form of insurance, shifting risk to the writer of the option. I am personally fascinated by the opportunities in these markets, including the Philadelphia options exchange in foreign currencies, and believe that they can be used to reduce risk for investors. The risk is thereby transferred to other market participants, who are willing to assume them, for a price. As long as the current cluster of uncertainties in the world continues and volatility in markets persists, I believe that options writing and trading will grow in importance.

Turning to the international situation, let us consider the LDC debt situation. First, the LDC debt situation provides some of the most frightening scenarios traders talk about. As on the nuclear question, traders fear that a serious miscalculation in Washington or in some other capitals could bring the whole international monetary system down. Second, although the central banks, the BIS, and even the IMF are to be given credit for their roles in avoiding a complete breakdown, up to this point the political leaders have dithered so much that they have aggravated the state of uncertainty. Investors really need clear leadership on these questions, starting with the United States. Up to now, the administration has spoken with many dissonant voices, and Congress has played reckless domestic politics with proposals that would only begin to deal with the LDC debt problem.

On the dollar, I will make three points. First, I am impressed with the volumes of capital that have flowed into the United States—into banks, the bond and stock markets, and real estate. Some of this money has been pulled into the United States and the dollar by the attraction of its high interest rates and by the depth and anonymity of its capital markets. Some of this money has been pushed into the dollar by market concerns over political and economic developments abroad. People the world over are scared, and the dollar is currently the world's main safe currency.

Second, I believe that the dollar has been pushed to levels that are much higher than would be justified on the basis of economic fundamentals. At the same time, however, competitive relationships are dynamic and we have to be careful with arguments that the dollar is seriously overvalued. As I said earlier, I detect that the complaints from U.S. industry are not as strong as they were, even in summer 1983. Perhaps the continuing revival of the domestic economy has helped some of these companies make sales at home that offset reduced orders from abroad. Perhaps the initial revival of growth in some other countries has helped some firms. And a few companies may have gotten what they wanted in Washington in the form of increased protection.

However, I wonder if another force is not at work—what we called in the 1970s the virtuous circle. At that time the appreciation of the German mark, Swiss franc, and Japanese yen cut the costs of raw material imports for those countries, reducing the costs of production and keeping their exports much more competitive than otherwise. The United States was caught in the vicious circle of a weakening dollar and rising inflation. Currently, U.S. firms are enjoying the benefits of low raw materials costs—particularly from the LDCs that are forced to produce and sell at low prices in order to service their debts. It is entirely possible that U.S. industry may not be losing as much ground competitively as it thinks.

If one country is in a virtuous circle, then one or more must be caught in a vicious circle. Some of the other major industrialized countries still have lower rates of inflation than the United States even though their currencies are declining against the dollar. Instead, the vicious circle counterpart would be the LDCs.

The third point is that the dollar's strength in the exchange market is nevertheless highly vulnerable. If the United States records a trade deficit on the order of $100 billion or more in 1984, as is forecast, it will have to attract even greater amounts of capital—through the pull and push processes I have outlined—than it did in 1983. Whenever the pace of the capital inflows slows, then the dollar could come under selling pressure.

Movements in dollar exchange rates, while erratic in both directions, have not been fully symmetrical. Most traders believe that the dollar should be lower if it were to trade only on the basis of fundamentals. But all traders have learned that each time they go short on the dollar something may happen—a rise in U.S. interest rates, an outbreak of hostilities in another area of the world, some renewed saber rattling by the USSR, a scare over the LDC debt, any of which suddenly propels funds into dollars. It is hard to build a position in anticipation of the kinds of shocks, many of which are political, that have led to surges in demand for dollars. When tensions relax, the dollar begins to ease off, and traders begin to build positions. Traders find that large positions either way are dangerous, however, and that the unwillingness to provide liquidity to the market has added to the volatility of exchange rates.

One of the current concerns of foreign exchange dealers in the interbank market is the trading behavior of the USSR's banking arm in London. Ask a trader why the dollar is up a particular morning and he or she is likely to answer, "The Russian bought dollars today." The USSR needs dollars to buy grain and other things in the West, but I have to believe that its current mode of operations is politically inspired. The Soviets can be very unobtrusive in markets when they want to be, even when they have big amounts to trade. They have proved this in their operations in gold and grain markets. Other market participants who have size to trade can do their business without anyone's hearing about it; the Saudi Arabians, for example, have been most professional on this score over the years. The tactics the "Russian" uses—calling a bank and buying $50 or $100 million on the wire—are sledgehammer blows to the market. The "Russian" was particularly active as a buyer of dollars after the USSR walked out of the Geneva talks on intermediate-range missiles. Traders can only guess why. Perhaps the Soviets want the dollar higher so they can get more for the gas and oil they sell to the West, to the extent that they might be paid in dollars for these exports. Perhaps they want the dollar higher so they can further embarrass our allies in Western Europe and Japan, as could be read into the dollar buying after the walkout in Geneva. Perhaps they want the dollar higher so they can place pressure on the governments of the LDCs that are struggling to solve their debt problems, igniting a revolution or two. I am not a kremlinologist, but I have been around long enough to know the signs of someone who is trying to bully the exchange market.

As you know, I have been an unflagging critic of the Reagan Administration's policy of nonintervention in the exchange market. The behavior of the "Russian" is another argument for the United States to resume cooperation with foreign authorities in the exchange market, including concerted and forceful intervention when it is needed. The Reagan Administration is programming billions of dollars to enhance the defenses of the Free World against every conceivable military threat the

Russians can raise. The administration has supplied counterpressure to Soviet adventurism in many areas of the world. However, in the defense of the Free World's international monetary system, the administration has chosen the course of unilateral disarmament. This course sounds far fetched to people who have not thought in these terms for the exchange market, but that is perhaps because the U.S. authorities have always been reluctant to discuss in public the strategic rationale for having a closely coordinated approach to the exchange markets with our allies in Western Europe and Japan.

A healthy international monetary system is important for the well-being of the Free World economy. The dollar is at the center of that system. The United States should provide more leadership than it has to assure that exchange rate relationships are fairly aligned to underlying conditions and that the exchange markets are reasonably orderly.

6
Effects of U.S. Economic Policy on Financial Markets

John D. Paulus

This chapter considers two related questions. First, to what extent have the governments of the developed nations been absorbing the savings of the private sector by running budget deficits, thereby retarding capital formation not only in the developed countries but also in the LDCs? Second, are the capital inflows into the United States a temporary cyclical phenomenon, or do they represent a longer-term trend whereby the United States will become a net absorber of capital from the rest of the world?

My conclusions are, first, that federal budget deficits in the developed countries have been absorbing a growing share of private sector savings. In the big seven OECD countries—Germany, Japan, the United Kingdom, Canada, France, Italy, and the United States—the absorption rate, which is the percentage of private savings absorbed by government budget deficits, has gone from around 10 percent in 1970 to over 50 percent in 1982. Not all of that increase is cyclical; much of it represents an increase in structural budget deficits in the major developed countries. Second, a series of monetary and fiscal policy actions in the United States has established a set of conditions under which that country may turn out to be a net absorber for a fairly extended period of time. Following is some of the reasoning behind these conclusions.

The extent to which budget deficits in developed countries are absorbing savings is an interesting question. If there is one thing that economists know, it is that to have investments, you have to have savings. Investment must be identically equal to savings, which does not mean that for every dollar of the budget deficit capital spending is necessarily reduced by a dollar. During recessions, deficits have the beneficial effects of sopping up savings and stimulating spending, thereby raising capacity utilization. During certain periods of the business cycle, deficits are not a bad thing. However, over the long run, budget deficits are not going to have much of an effect on the level of economic activity. What they do is affect the composition of economic output. Big budget deficits tend to encourage consumer spending and to discourage capital spending. Less capital means slower capital formation and lower long-run growth potential for the world. Government budget deficits affect capital formation not only in the countries that run the deficits, the developed countries, but also in the rest of the world as well because financial markets are pretty tightly integrated.

Table 6–1 shows the percentage of central government budget deficits to net private savings in the OECD countries, which account for 73 percent of Free World output. During the 1960s, the absorption rate was relatively low and fairly stable. Between 5 and 10 percent of the net private savings available for private capital formation was used to finance federal budget deficits. From 1970 onward, there was a decisive upward trend in the absorption rate. In 1975, for example, the absorption rate

Table 6–1
Central Government Deficit (–) or Surplus of the Big Seven OECD Countries as a Percentage of Net Private Savings, 1960–1982

Year	Deficit
1960	– 2.7%
1961	– 6.9
1962	– 8.8
1963	– 7.5
1964	– 6.8
1965	– 4.7
1966	– 6.9
1967	– 10.9
1968	– 12.1
1969	1.5
1970	– 6.7
1971	– 13.6
1972	– 11.8
1973	– 8.3
1974	– 10.8
1975	– 36.4
1976	– 24.9
1977	– 27.0
1978	– 33.3
1979	– 29.7
1980	– 39.3
1981	– 42.7
1982	– 57.1

Sources: The 1960–1977 net private savings were obtained from the United Nations' 1980 *Yearbook of National Accounts Statistics* and federal budget deficits from the 1983 *International Financial Statistics Yearbook* published by the International Monetary Fund. For 1978–1982 both net private savings and federal budget deficits were obtained from the 1983 *World Economic Outlook* published by the International Monetary Fund.

Note: The Big Seven OECD countries are Canada, France, Germany, Italy, Japan, the United Kingdom, and the United States.

went from over 10 percent to a little over 36 percent. Part of the increase was cyclical, related to the worldwide recession of 1974 to 1975, but the fact that the absorption rate did not fall back to previous levels after 1975 implies that much of the increase was structural. This was certainly the case in the United States as is demonstrated in the following.

By 1980, on the eve of the last major synchronous recession, the governments of the OECD countries were absorbing about 40 percent of the net savings in those countries. With the recession, the absorption rate has gone higher, rising to 57 percent in 1982. While it is true that much of the increase reflects weak economic conditions around the world, much of it also reflects a rise in structural budget deficits around the world. By *structural*, we mean the budget deficits that would be obtained under full employment.

Table 6-2 shows the structural budget deficit as a percentage of GNP for the period of 1955 to 1985. The structural budget deficit is not exactly unprecedented. There was a structural budget deficit of 3.1 percent in 1967. In fact, it is interesting to look at what happened to the structural budget deficit from 1960 to 1967 because it reflects the fiscal policy of the Kennedy/Johnson years. It hit 2.7 percent in 1975. There was a very big swing in fiscal policy in 1975, when there were $50 rebates for everybody. But the difference between those isolated cases and the situation today is that the recent very large structural budget deficits are essentially permanent.

The structural budget deficit in the United States in 1983 was about $100 billion, 3 percent of GNP. In 1984 estimates are that it will be $130 billion, and in 1985, $140 billion, roughly 3.5 percent of GNP. Using the estimate by the Council of Economic Advisors for 1983, which puts the

Table 6-2
The Structural Budget Deficit (−) or Surplus of the United States as a Percentage of GNP, 1955–1985

Year	Deficit	Year	Deficit	Year	Deficit
1955	− 0.3%	1965	− 1.2%	1975	− 2.7%
1956	0.1	1966	− 2.1	1976	− 2.0
1957	0	1967	− 3.1	1977	− 2.1
1958	− 0.9	1968	− 2.3	1978	− 1.6
1959	0.5	1969	− 0.4	1979	− 0.8
1960	1.5	1970	− 1.1	1980	− 1.3
1961	0.5	1971	− 1.6	1981	− 0.8
1962	− 0.4	1972	− 1.5	1982	− 2.1
1963	0	1973	− 1.2	1983	− 3.1
1964	− 1.1	1974	− 0.5	1984	− 3.5
				1985	− 3.4

Note: Figures for 1984 and 1985 are Morgan Stanley Economic Research estimates.

structural U.S. budget deficit at $210 billion, and assuming that nominal GNP grows by about 10 percent a year, the structural budget deficit in 1988 would be 4 percent of GNP.

To put that figure into perspective, the net savings pool in the developed world is around a trillion dollars. The U.S. structural deficit is approaching $150 billion by 1985 and over $200 billion by 1988. That means that the structural deficit is absorbing roughly 15 percent of the net savings pool. To put it into another perspective, the deficits in the OECD countries were close to $500 billion in 1983, while lending to LDCs varied between $50 and $30 billion dollars from 1976 to 1982. The governments of the developed countries are absorbing 10 times the amount of what has been loaned to the Third World of the world's scarce savings. This is the largest drain on savings in history, and it will have important negative implications for capital formation not only in the developed countries but also in the LDCs.

The second question to be covered is relatively related to the first. Are the recent capital inflows into the United States the result of temporary cyclical factors, or are they indicative of a longer-term trend that will turn the United States into an absorber of capital from the rest of the world? The United States, perhaps unwittingly, has adopted a net of financial policies that could produce capital inflows into the United States for a long period of time. There are some obvious reasons why the United States has been the recipient of recent capital inflows. For example, U.S. recovery is ahead of the rest of the world, and this recovery has attracted a lot of dollar IOUs from the rest of the world. U.S. budget deficits are large and growing, and this factor has tended to hold U.S. real interest rates up, making dollar investments attractive. However, U.S. real interest rates are about 400 basis points higher than a trade-weighted average of real interest rates of the major trading partners of the United States. The 400-basis-point advantage has made the dollar investments so attractive and has held the dollar up, resulting in capital inflows into the United States. At most it is believed that U.S. budget deficits might raise U.S. real rates by a couple hundred basis points, which means that only part of the differential can be blamed on U.S. fiscal policy.

It is not correct to say that the United States has been pursuing a policy of easy fiscal policy and tight money, resulting in high real interest rates, because the United States is not pursuing a tight monetary policy. High real interest rates have been caused by a combination of the deregulation of the U.S. financial system, which has put a heavy burden on interest rates in rationing credit, a heavier burden than in most other developed countries, and the U.S. tax system, which is quite generous for borrowers and rather severe for lenders. Foreign investors like such high interest rates.

Before the United States deregulated its financial system, the intermediation process was essentially hamstrung from time to time, especially when interest rates rose above Regulation Q ceilings. In fact, the intermediation process was crippled during periods when interest rates went above Regulation Q ceilings. Basically, that is equivalent to blowing up factories. When the system of intermediation is prevented from working, less GNP will be produced for a given level of interest rates; that is, it takes a lower level of interest rates to produce a given level of GNP when the system is under fairly tight financial regulation.

Consider, for example, 1974. Interest rates were above Regulation Q ceilings. There was a pretty substantial disintermediation. The United States blew up a lot of factories, in effect, and produced an economic contraction with 12 percent inflation, 12 percent nominal interest rates, no real rates, and substantially negative real after-tax rates. The ceilings are gone now. This regulatory network began to be dismantled in 1978. In 1980, 1981, and 1982, the economy experienced 12 percent inflation again. This time it took a rate of 20 percent to produce the same kind of contraction as in 1974. The United States had substantially positive real rates of 800 basis points. Why 20 percent, though? Why not 15? That is where the tax system comes in. The United States has a very liberal tax system for borrowers and a severe system for lenders in that virtually all interest can be deducted by the borrower from his or her taxes. That is important because a substantial percentage of borrowing and lending in the United States is done by sectors for whom taxes are an important consideration.

Table 6–3 gives the borrowing and lending figures for the sectors for whom taxes are not an important consideration, such as state and local governments, foreigners, and pension funds. These sectors only accounted for between 10 and 20 percent of all the borrowing and lending done in U.S. capital markets. Thus, between 80 and 90 percent of all borrowing and lending was done by sectors for whom taxes are an important consideration. The pattern is different in most other developed countries. The United States has a higher price percentage of borrowers and lenders who can use the tax system. This means that real interest rates are not a good measure of the degree of tightness in monetary policy. Real after-tax interest rates are what matters for the great bulk of borrowers and lenders.

Many analyses show an estimate of real after-tax bond rates in the United States. Inflationary expectations were estimated using a 5-year weighted average of past inflation. The figures lead to the conclusion that present real after-tax bond rates with inflationary expectations of about 6 percent are close to 0. Thus, a 11.5 percent long government bond may be issued at 50 basis points above that—say, 12 percent. After taxes the return would be about 7, which is a point or so above expected

Table 6-3
Borrowing and Lending by Nontaxable Sectors, 1955–1982
($ billions)

Borrowing and Lending	1955–1959	1960–1964	1965–1969	1970–1974	1975–1979	1980–1982
Private Sector Borrowing						
Total borrowing	37.0	52.0	82.7	156.9	282.7	320.1
State and local governments	5.1	5.8	8.5	14.4	16.7	31.8
Foreign	1.0	2.5	2.9	6.7	19.6	23.3
Subtotal	6.0	8.2	11.4	21.2	36.4	55.1
Percentage of total	16.4	15.8	13.8	13.5	12.9	17.2
Private Sector Lending						
Total lending	36.9	52.3	80.0	160.5	319.0	398.3
State and local governments	0.9	1.0	2.6	2.1	11.3	26.8
Foreign	1.1	0.9	0.1	11.4	18.9	19.3
Private and pension funds	1.6	1.9	1.5	1.5	8.0	14.7
State and local retirement funds	1.5	2.3	3.4	4.9	11.8	21.2
Subtotal	5.2	6.0	7.6	19.8	50.0	82.0
Percentage of total	14.0	11.5	9.4	12.4	15.7	20.6

inflation. Real after-tax borrowing costs today are not very different than what they were in the 1950s, and the first part of the 1960s. They are higher than they were in the 1970s, but that is precisely the time period that should not be used as a standard of comparison with today's interest rates because the 1970s were substantially influenced by the network of regulatory ceilings, which are gone now. Today's rates should be compared with the 1950s and 1960s when though there were ceilings, they were generally far enough above interest rates so they really did not impede the intermediation process.

Thus, the combination of substantial financial market deregulation and a generous tax system has produced very high real interest rates in this country that, for foreigners, make for very attractive per dollar investment, but these real interest rates are relatively irrelevant to the United States. Real after-tax interest rates are a better measure of financial stringency, and they are not very high currently. It is not a combination of easy fiscal and tight monetary policy that is bringing capital into this country but more of a combination of a substantially deregulated financial system and a very liberal tax system, which is producing the capital inflows and which I suspect will continue to produce them for an extended period of time.

Regarding the absorption of savings by governments in the developed countries, on an efficiency basis, this growing absorption rate is retarding capital formation and slowing the long-run growth potential of our economy. On an equity basis, the major losers are probably the LDCs where the truly poor in this world live. The deficits in the developing countries are diverting capital away from the LDCs, and the numbers are staggering. The whole LDC debt outstanding right now is over $600 billion, a figure that is about equal to the amount of growth in the government debt of the developed countries in 1983.

Regarding the question of capital inflows, some of these inflows are financing U.S. consumption through the budget deficit. However, some are financing capital spending. The United States has a comparative advantage in the production of certain high-technology capital goods such as microprocessors, computers, tape drives, and radar. It is devoting one-third of business fixed investment spending to high-tech capital goods, over $100 billion a year for computers, telecommunications equipment, and so on. Given the composition of the U.S. work force, 50 percent of the work force is working where the capital-labor ratios are relatively low. I do not have much capital applied to me—a desk, some lights, a pencil, and some paper—but the potential for increasing productivity in this one-half of the work force by applying better capital in terms of word processors, computers, and similar equipment is substantial. In this way, the potential possibly justifies some of these capital inflows into the United States. It does seem strange to think of the world's largest and probably most developed economy absorbing capital from the rest of the world, but I think that is the way it will be for an extended period.

7

Foreign Exchange Markets: A Corporate Perspective

Jon W. Rotenstreich

The turbulence in the financial markets of the past 10 years has certainly created an interesting background for economic historians. In addition to the dislocations and volatility, it has produced an extraordinary example of financial adjustment and innovation. The changes in the capital markets have been the manifestation of vast changes in attitudes by the savings system worldwide as well as by governments and private sector demanders of funds.

A major theme of this period has been the notion of *risk transfer.* The period of volatility and uncertainty has given birth to a new industry within the financial marketplace—the segmentation and identification of various types of risks, the securitization of these risks, and the pricing and redistribution of them.

First, I describe some of the reasons for this process in the savings sector—the supply side of the equation—and then project the direction this process has placed upon the investment sector, at least from a corporate perspective. The foreign exchange markets will be the crucible where a major confluence of this risk transfer process will be and, to some extent, is being felt.

A major process affecting savings over the past 25 years is undoubtedly institutionalization. The 1960s saw extraordinary growth of an industry of equity-oriented fund managers. For example, the mutual fund industry began to harness large amounts of previously fragmented savings flows from individuals all over the United States. At the same time, an even greater force was becoming intrigued with equity investments— the private pensions. Each of these events had a common objective: to seek higher real returns.

Another force in the savings process has been the impact of rapacious inflation. Coming on the heels of the institutionalization and homogenization in thinking in the savings process, inflation and stagflation accelerated the demand for performance-oriented investment. Investment horizons since 1974 have been shortened and the depth of fixed income markets lessened to preserve capital and to meet the unexpected opportunities constantly available to a highly volatile market. No longer are returns compared with historical results, but investment returns increasingly take on a comparative performance with other investors. Indeed, speculation has become institutionalized.

This measurement drive in the savings industry has, as its latest manifestation, opportunity cost as the principal standard. Bond returns are compared with stock returns and with collectibles and are ultimately measured by the geography or currency of ownership. There is a naive notion of total transferability of assets among these categories at will, and long-term objectives are in some way less important. We will all be dead in the long run, to take a little poetic license, if we continue to embrace short-term performance at the expense of sound long-term objectives. Is the spot liquidation price of the assets of a company, as demanded by arbitrageurs and money managers, the best value for the stockholders? A long discussion of this point is off the general subject, but the measurement drive has been an important aspect of capital market development over the past few years.

Today the investment management problem is increasingly worldwide in focus. In addition, the investment management focus is increasingly independent of tax considerations. Meanwhile, corporate capital is beginning to feel the pressure of this opportunity cost focus. At one end of the spectrum is the corporate liquidation question. Are the corporate assets invested to their highest returns? At the other end of the spectrum is the financial risk and opportunity identification and the rebalancing of those risks.

During the period that the investment of savings evolved from a historical return orientation through a comparative return orientation and now to an opportunity cost measurement, corporate finance was somewhat immune. It really was not until the early part of the 1980s that innovation and change became accepted as reasonable solutions to corporate financial problems. Familiar examples are the zero coupon bond, bond warrants, financial futures, and other innovations of this period.

The most significant development has been the fact that financing risks can be segmented and dealt with individually. The key elements of financing decisions are price, timing, quantity, and currency. Through various hedging techniques, the pricing can be deferred, timing repositioned, even quantity changed and currency exposure shifted.

The securitization of maturity risk, the zero coupon bond, has become the medium through which various corporate financing risks can be dealt with. For example, after an extended debate by accountants, defeasance, the removal of debt from the balance sheet before it is either callable or feasible to call, can be accomplished effectively using zero coupon bonds or U.S. Treasury stripped bonds as a proxy.

The securitization of timing, financial futures, can create accelerated access to the capital markets or a deferral of pricing. In addition, hedges can be from the long side as well as the short side, allowing funding to take place independent of pricing. Likewise, bond warrants allow for interest rate exposures to be moderated, controlled, or accelerated.

The attractiveness of each of these new vehicles to the corporate treasurer lies in a montage of risk segmentation instruments. The appropriate mix can articulate the level of exposure for any issuer or investor. Consider, for instance, the simple combination of a U.S. dollar borrowing with warrants to buy deutsche marks. The corporate treasurer might then approach the foreign exchange market and purchase an option to buy deutsche marks at a specified rate. If the deutsche mark improves vis-à-vis the dollar, the treasurer exercises the option, takes the gain, and reduces the U.S. dollar cost. He or she then lends deutsche marks to his or her German subsidiary on a cost-effective basis. Assuming the deutsche mark declines in value vis-à-vis the dollar, the treasurer merely lets his or her option expire, absorbs the cost of the option, converts spot to deutsche marks, and lends deutsche marks at a much more attractive level. All of this, of course, assumes continued volatility.

The entry and growth of a broad class of speculators in the capital markets has provided an increased array of financing strategies for the treasurer. Furthermore, these tools can be used on a continuous basis. The marketability of these new securitized risks allows for hedges to be taken, removed, and otherwise adjusted continuously. A drawback, of course, is the taxability of gains and losses on hedges, but I predict that as the process becomes more prevalent, tax relief will be forthcoming.

Foreign exchange is the result of interest rate differentials and forces that affect investor perception—political and social as well as economic. These risks are also segmented by our new capital markets and allow the corporate treasurer to reexamine the way in which he or she previously dealt with these questions.

For example, a foreign subsidiary was traditionally thought to be best capitalized by borrowing as much local currency as necessary to support local operations. The long-term measurement became the net profit after fully accounting for foreign exchange exposure of all expenses. Insofar as the foreign assets of the company were weighted by the foreign liabilities, the process of indexing both earnings and assets of the company in the foreign currency was dealt with in one financing policy.

Today it is possible to capitalize a foreign subsidiary on a basis consistent with local financing objectives while maintaining a different currency exposure at the parent level. FAS-52 has provided that a hedge of foreign assets can be implemented without accounting for the volatility of foreign exchange through the income statement. This rule reintroduces the opportunity of asset management or capital management as a strategic focus for multinational corporations.

The use of long-term forwards, futures, and options will proliferate. The zero sum nature of the short-term foreign exchange markets may give way to an increased awareness of longer periods of exposure management. In effect, in addition to the present focus on dividends, cash flows, and manufacturing- or marketing-related foreign exchange opportunities, a longer-term asset management focus on foreign exchange will increasingly evolve.

Other risks also might be segmented within each country's financial structure. Floating rates under certain conditions, for one, may partially counteract the impact of foreign exchange volatility. Therefore, a close analysis of the correlation between foreign exchange and floating rate instruments may prove worthy of different financing or investment strategies.

It is very difficult in any investment market to predict outcomes. However, each investor has a different risk profile, and by isolating risk exposure and rebuilding portfolios predicated on a composite of manageable risks, the Monte Carlo outcome may be more in line with management expectations. Uncertainty will continue to dominate, but a rational method for dealing with risks must be incorporated into financial planning.

The investor, of course, is the other side of the financing entity. The private sector has been driven primarily by earnings performance. As asset focus proliferates, the corporate treasurer will spend more time thinking about continuous opportunity cost, asset mobilization, asset life, liability management, and the general subject of risk transfer and manageable risks. The treasurer will indeed be a portfolio manager of his or her corporate assets.

IBM has used some of these techniques with respect to liability management. In August 1981, IBM hedged, through the use of long-term forward contracts with the World Bank, two Swiss franc and deutsche mark loans that had originally been borrowed in April 1980. By buying these forwards, IBM locked in its U.S. dollar cost of borrowing. In effect, what happened is that in 1980 IBM borrowed intermediate-term Swiss francs and deutsche marks. It converted the spot of 1.76 and 2.18 to dollars. In 1981, the Swiss franc spot was 2.18, and the deutsche mark was 2.58. At that point, IBM bought forward the Swiss franc and deutsche mark necessary to repay all interest and principal. Thus, IBM, in 1980, needed funding and decided that the Swiss franc and deutsche mark provided the best opportunity cost medium. IBM continued to need the funding but was able to isolate the foreign exchange risk and deal with it independently of the funding.

Earlier in 1980 IBM was able to borrow Canadian dollars efficiently by borrowing in the U.S. Eurodollar market and simultaneously hedge the interest and principal so that a synthetic Canadian borrowing was effected. These techniques are now very popular. The interesting fact is that the tombstones in the *Financial Times* are not necessarily the total picture of the transactions that have been arranged.

Furthermore, the use of options on foreign exchange opens the way to some very interesting strategies with regard to product sourcing and marketing. For example, if a product is imported from country A to country B, the product manager may decide to hedge the ultimate contract price. Conversely, he or she may decide to purchase an option in an attempt to optimize price. In any event, not considering elimination of the currency risk with the many tools available is to increase risk unnecessarily. Managing the risk is the key. In some situations a forward position is more desirable, and in others an option is more efficacious. The choice depends on the degree of risk that an investor is prepared to embrace.

I shall now discuss briefly IBM and international capital management. IBM operates a decentralized financial system. Its primary thrust is to maintain and increase productivity in each of its 41 manufacturing locations around the world. IBM's desire to improve productivity in these countries is expressed in its desire to increase investment in its people as well as plant.

In 1983, IBM invested $2 billion in research and development. It invested $2.4 billion in 1983 and over $10 billion in capital expansion over the last 5 years. More important, IBM is dedicated to enlarging its investment in the education and training of its employees worldwide because capital, people, and management work together to produce productivity. The desire to continue to invest despite market volatility has been one of the factors that has helped to maintain and improve IBM's growth and productivity.

IBM's method of dealing in foreign exchange is very simple. It operates a multilateral foreign-exchange-netting system to eliminate duplicate transactions. Otherwise, the corporate treasurer sets policy with respect to foreign exchange exposure for the subsidiary countries. IBM's transactions are associated with the flow of cash from operations on a decentralized basis. Occasionally, IBM has used longer-term forwards to execute a specific longer-term objective.

The interrelationship between dollar markets and nondollar markets and increased volatility of interest rates and currency and the proliferation of these new risk management tools may provide new opportunities to balance and manage those risks in a prudent manner. IBM's principal financing objective is to maintain capital availability, and its primary business thrust is to continue to have the longer-term view of increasing productivity in all its international locations. Productivity can be achieved through increased investment. IBM hopes these new financial tools will assist it in meeting its objectives.

8
Capital Markets: Prospects for Long-Term Investments

Pedro Pablo Kuczynski

The United States is clearly in the middle of a transition. There is nothing new about that transition on several fronts, but the country seems to be moving at a fairly rapid pace into three changes. The first one is a much less regulated environment, not only in the United States but also in other markets, where distinction between various types of financial institutions are becoming increasingly blurred. In the United States, the distinction between brokerage and banking, widely defined, is tending to diminish, and geographic distinctions among commercial banks are also disappearing.

Second, what is not clear is whether the United States is in a transition toward a permanently higher level of interest rates as a result of deregulation and whether that will be accompanied by a long period of lower growth. Certainly, the symptoms in 1983 suggest not, but the question of long-term growth prospects goes unanswered.

The third change is the substantial political uncertainty in East-West relationships, and perhaps less evident is a period of what could be very substantial tensions between North and South, particularly in Latin America. How do these changes affect long-term markets?

The answer to this question involves four major issues. The first issue is the U.S. policy mix between a budget deficit and a countervailing monetary policy that has tended to have an effect on long-term rates, which are very high in real terms. The second issue is institutional change, changes in the laws and in the way of doing business. The third issue is industrial restructuring, which is clearly of great importance both in the United States and in Europe. Finally, the fourth is the impact on markets of the Latin American debt question and to some degree the debt problems of other LDCs.

Concerning the fiscal and monetary policy mix, it is fairly clear that while there is much concern about the U.S. budget deficit in the press, so far it seems to be much less harmful than might be expected, but that is largely due to the stage of the economic cycle in which the country finds itself. At this stage of the cycle, companies are highly profitable because they are gradually eating into their excess capacity, and this, like any expansion, is very profitable from the point of view of a cash flow and net income.

At the same time, companies find themselves in a bull market on equities so their capital-raising functions have tended to emphasize equity rather than going to the bond market. In any case, they did not need to go to the bond market because they had, as a result of the wrenching recession, already put their balance sheets in order over the last two or three years. Thus, currently (February 1984) the crowding-out worries do not seem to be justified. However, that does not mean that the problem might not arise if any of the elements change. As the recovery goes on and excess capacity falls so that funding needs for plant improvement and expansion increase, there may be very substantial uncertainties in the markets, particularly if the attractiveness of the equity market starts to diminish, as it quite probably will, given time.

Another factor is that by international standards, the U.S. public sector deficit, at about 4 to 5 percent of GNP, is low if one compares it to the total savings available to finance it, which obviously include foreign savings. U.S. domestic disposable savings, as is well known, are not high. However, with the present policy mix and the attractiveness of the flow of funds into the United States, the deficit is not high in relation to the flow of funds into the country. As the other industrialized countries begin to recover, and certainly the outlook in Europe for 1984 tends to be encouraging in that respect, the available funds that are flowing into the United States could fall off at the margin. Therefore, some of the concerns about the continuing U.S. budget deficit may well materialize. The policy mix currently tends to take advantage of the cyclical circumstances, which are highly favorable to the financing of large public sector needs, but significant elements of uncertainty remain that depend on the pace of recovery elsewhere and on the nature of the recovery in the United States.

The issue of deregulation is a major area of transition and uncertainty. Clearly, deregulation has had major positive effects as is shown by the mushrooming growth of the Eurobond market in the last three or four years, which in terms of new corporate issues caught up with the U.S. market in 1982. In that period it grew at about three times the rate of the U.S. domestic bond market. Deregulation has certainly stimulated growth in financial instruments, and there is no reason to doubt that this tendency will continue if deregulation does not stop or reverse.

However, some significant dangers in deregulation exist. One indirect danger is the growth of organizations that become, in essence, financial conglomerates, running insurance companies, mutual funds, foreign exchange, bond portions, loan portfolios, door-to-door sales of securities, and so on. These organizations could over time, unless very stringent internal controls are successfully implemented, run into the problems that some of the conglomerates ran into in the golden age of industrial conglomeration 20 years ago.

There are, as a result of the new environment, some dynamic areas of growth in the markets. Probably the two most significant areas are the growth of securities trading and the issuance of collateralized mortgage obligations, which today account for about 30 percent of the trading in securities in the major U.S. markets. That figure can be contrasted with the situation of 3 or 4 years ago when mortgage securities were a very small proportion of the total. These new securities structure the commercial and interest risks in innovative ways and have gained large-scale international acceptance. Whether this rapid growth will go on at the tremendous pace of the last 2 or 3 years remains somewhat uncertain. With hedging and swaps, both of currencies and interest rates, the authority of both commercial and investment banks is growing rapidly.

Another area in deregulation concerns the U.S. withholding tax on interest paid to foreigners other than governments and central banks. A bill to remove this tax is being considered by Congress, but it is unclear whether this bill will prosper or not. If it were to gain approval it would have significant implications for the Eurobond market by eliminating the tax advantage for U.S. corporation dollar issues in Europe and by making it more attractive for foreign institutions to switch to U.S. Treasury paper. Removal of the tax could create a substantial flow of funds into the Treasury market and might also affect dramatically the way in which the bonds are priced internationally. This would tend to accentuate more than now the flight toward quality that one sees in most markets today and would tend to augment the differentials between Treasury rates and what other private borrowers have to say.

In the area of industrial restructuring, the United States faces a number of substantial uncertainties because it is not entirely clear to what extent industries such as steel, copper, and the refining of basic metals are in a long-term decline or whether they are facing simply a cyclical decline that will gradually work itself out. As companies have reduced wages, they have very sharply reduced their costs. It seems that in these same industries, the industrialized economies are losing their comparative advantage. There is a point beyond which technology cannot offset wage and other social-related costs, so that there is an increasing shift of such industries to developing countries that by themselves may not be very efficient producers but that, for one reason or another, have lower raw material costs and certainly much lower wage costs. Japan has shown the way in industrial restructuring. They very quietly have shut down a major portion of their aluminum industry, for example, and are now in the process of shutting down some of the other basic metals industries.

In the United States and in Europe there has been more difficulty in doing that. For the financial markets, the result of this trend has been the growth of the market for high-yield, or junk, bonds, which are priced at a very attractive yield to the investor. Part of the market is always interested in such paper, and that market is booming, particularly for steel company paper.

Let me turn to the developing countries. In terms of bond markets, their relevance is exceedingly limited. The time when some of the Latin American countries will be able to issue fixed rate paper in the major markets is far away. However, it is worth pointing out that the service on these bonds has been punctually kept so that sort of paper is quite attractive to investors. Countries like Mexico will do everything to maintain the service on their outstanding bonded debt.

Concerning the problem of developing country debt, I think the emphasis is wrong. The emphasis should really be on the long-term political aspects of the problem, particularly for the Latin American countries. It is not really sustainable for an area as large as Latin America, with a growth rate in its labor force of close to 3 percent a year, to sustain for very long income declines of the size suffered since 1981. I emphasize income rather than GNP because of the terms of trade effect, which is substantial. For the Latin American region as a whole, per capita income by the end of 1983 had fallen at least 12 percent compared to 1981, and worse yet, almost all of this income fall has involved the lower income groups. The potential volatility of continuing the present pattern, under which countries have to pay about 45 to 50 percent of their export earnings in interest, can only be very high. I think the markets have already discounted it in a considerable degree. The danger is more to the debtor countries than to the leaders, on which attention has been focused. Reserves exist for such eventualities, although earnings would obviously take a loss if something were to happen. The real problem is that the economic and political outlooks of many of these countries would deteriorate rather dramatically. There is some hope at the end of the tunnel if the determination of the debtors to adjust is accompanied by a hospitable external environment, including lower interest rates and a lower valued dollar. The debtors have the human material resources to work themselves out of the problem, albeit slowly at first.

Part IV
Adjustment and Austerity Policies in the Developing Countries

9

Industrialized Country Policies and Financing Adjustment in the Developing Countries

C. David Finch

The World Economic Outlook

An economist is expected to describe the consequences of certain events or policies, but the policymakers who act in a political environment determine the evolution of events. Perhaps economists can try to guide people toward improving the outcome based on technical analysis, but in no sense can they prescribe. In today's environment one should expect less than ideal solutions to problems that are very complex, but it is critically important that a well-grounded attempt be made to identify clearly the direction of change.

What are the main elements of recent developments and the economic outlook? First, it is quite clear that the global economic situation was better at the end of 1983 than it was at the time of the IMF's Annual Meeting in Toronto at the end of August 1982. There has been an important recovery in the United States, and it has been more rapid than anticipated. It has now become clear that Europe is also poised for better growth. Overall industrialized country growth is expected to be over the critical minimum figure of 3 percent that is usually quoted in public discussions. These are positive developments because they provide some breathing space for policymakers to develop long-term solutions to encourage a lasting and balanced economic recovery.

Second, there have been important improvements on the developing countries' side. Some analysts say that the developing countries have yet to face their balance of payments problems. This is not true; in the developing countries there has been a very major adjustment, and they have, in fact, lived for almost 2 years now with the changed situation. From the middle of 1982, when bank lending slowed dramatically, developing countries have faced difficulty in maintaining the growth of imports. Among many of the major borrowers in the developing countries, imports came down abruptly and sharply in a sort of forced balance of payments adjustment.

Third, as a result of the events of the past 2 years, the international financial community has learned to work together, and this cooperation has been critical in the functioning of the world financial system. The biggest part has undoubtedly been played by the BIS collection of central banks. The main central banks, the main supervisors of the commercial banks—the people who meet in the Cooke Committee—and the BIS have worked together in a very constructive way to meet the problems.

I make a special point of these developments because they are easily overlooked, given that the same set of events is viewed differently by participants with many diverse interests. It is true that, in Europe, the first problems to be perceived were those with the Eastern European countries. At the time, it looked as if the United States was a little less than interested in cooperating with Europe to deal with the financial difficulties of Eastern Europe. Thus, the Europeans, when they saw the difficulties in Latin America, might have been reluctant to reciprocate. In the event these fears were unfounded, a certain coherent approach was developed to the debt problems of Latin America, and the coherence was not limited to the central banks. Commercial banks throughout the world have been equally responsive and have reacted together to the difficult situations of the recent past. This was an important positive step in international financial cooperation.

Perhaps even more important, the developing countries, when faced with this situation, did not react politically. They did not repudiate the debts and were willing to work with the rest of the world to cope with their difficulties. They also have been working with the IMF in trying to ease the problems. A major example of cooperation is the case of Mexico. Other countries have similarly extended the same cooperation.

An objective view also requires recognition of the clouds on the horizon. The cooperation and the onset of economic recovery have provided additional time. In the future, the world faces a long period of relatively slower growth. The rapid growth of the 1960s and early 1970s is not going to be easily recreated. The world will have to be tolerant of slow growth, but this will be possible politically only if there is a shared sense of better control over events and a clear sense of direction.

Industrialized Country Policies

Against this background, what are the main policy issues in the industrialized countries? The most important issue is undoubtedly the problem of the fiscal deficit, particularly in the United States. There is no question that the United States, by its growing structural deficit, is crowding out the possibilities of productive investment within the United States and limiting the prospect for widening the capital base in the developing countries. There is no doubt how investors would react if given the alternatives of buying U.S. Treasury bills at a high rate of return or investing in Brazil or Mexico given the problems. This pressure on financial markets of the U.S. deficit is a great source of concern not only because of its impact on the growth prospects of the poor parts of the world but also because of the consequences to the United States. The interest bill on U.S. government debt, if it bears more and more heavily on future U.S. budget deficits, adds cumulatively to gaps with which the United States must somehow deal.

There is another aspect of the problem of fiscal deficits. The United States, in effect, is beginning to borrow very heavily from abroad, which may ultimately lead to its role as a reserve center being questioned. There is a danger that at some stage this heavy borrowing could lead to exchange rate instability. At present, the deficit is clearly drawing the exchange rate out of line with what would be warranted by considerations of trade competitiveness. The inflow of exchange that is encouraged by the high real interest rates in the United States is pushing the exchange rate higher, making the steel and other trade problems worse and jeopardizing employment in many export industries and manufacturing. It is only by tackling the fiscal problems that ultimately the United States will be in a position to pursue open trade policies and depend less on capital inflows.

Of course, this is not just a U.S. problem. Europe also has its fiscal deficits, which have drifted upward over the last 10 years. These countries are all faced with the struggle to bring the budget deficits into line with realities for the long-term future. The problems of coping with the budget, the slow growth of real income, and the heightened rate of unemployment have led in the industrialized countries to the problem of increased protectionism, to which I return at the end of the chapter.

Financing and Adjustment in Developing Countries: The Role of the IMF

I have indicated that the developing countries have dealt with the external deficits in the sense that the gap in the balance of payments has been reduced. But that does not mean that the economic problems are being solved; rather, in many cases, the balance of payments squeeze is being transmitted into severe domestic problems. Inflation rates are accelerating in many developing countries. Brazil's annual rate of inflation in the last four months of 1983 was close to 300 percent. This is destructive of any economic system, even with the best system of indexation. Argentina is experiencing inflation even higher than that of Brazil. Mexico has struggled to reduce inflation and has done a good job so far by reducing it from nearly 100 percent in 1982 to 55 percent in 1983. The inflationary pressures still exist, however, and the authorities are pressing to reduce them.

Another symptom of the extreme stress being experienced by these countries is the extraordinarily high rate of unemployment. Of course, there are also unemployment problems in the industrialized countries, but the developing countries have much less of a social security safety net and fewer mechanisms for coping with the social costs of unemployment. Unemployment rates are also much worse in these countries than in the industrialized countries.

There is thus no doubt that the countries that had been dependent on foreign borrowing are presently suffering far more than anybody else in the world. This fact poses a danger for the coherence of the world economy by encouraging a shift in these countries toward inward-looking policies. It also jeopardizes the possibilities of resuming a normal growth rate that is undoubtedly feasible, given the extent to which technology has evolved in the world. Higher growth rates depend on adequate flows of resources and on the availability of opportunities for the efficient use of resources.

The IMF is sometimes caricatured as "cracking the whip." In fact, these developing countries are doing what they feel they have to do in the light of world conditions. The adjustment problems of these countries exist and have to be dealt with whether the IMF is there or not. Brazil experienced a slow or negative rate of growth for a number of years before there was an IMF program. In instituting its program, Brazil was merely reacting to the need to prove its adjustment effort in a more orderly way. The association of the IMF with the Brazilian adjustment effort came when Brazil's need for funds became acute and there was need for a special effort to raise extra funds.

The IMF's role in these countries is simply to try to get as much order into the events as possible. It strengthens the hands of the finance ministry and those elements in the government that are trying to see that the consequences of the difficult world situation are being properly anticipated and that whatever a government can do to ease the difficulties is being done.

The IMF is truly committed to working with the countries to come to an orderly resolution of their budgetary problems. Mexico has made a major effort by cutting its fiscal deficit from 18 to 8.5 percent of gross domestic product (GDP). The importance and difficulty of a reduction of this magnitude cannot be overemphasized; in the United States, for example, there are difficulties with a reduction of 1 percent, even on a contingency basis.

When a country like Brazil is faced with financing problems, it is quite clear that, without some organized effort, the banks would naturally withdraw much of their short-term capital. It is also clear that most of the export credit agencies in the rest of the world, faced with delays or refinancing questions, would want to cut off their credits or to limit them. It is thus evident that a country needs to mobilize all the official support it can to avoid a rapid loss of external resources.

One of the first levels of official support is the IMF. Unfortunately, the amounts the IMF can handle—basically determined by the lending countries—are relatively small. Brazil again illustrates this point. The amount the IMF can provide in 1 year to Brazil is 15 percent of their 1983 interest payments to the rest of the world. Such an amount cannot change the situation dramatically, let alone bail out the banks. The amount is in no sense on the scale originally intended for the IMF, which was intended to ease a country's problems significantly when its balance of payments abruptly got into difficulties. But of course it is useful. It eases the transition. Most important, even though the IMF only provides a relatively small proportion of the financing, IMF involvement encourages a contribution from other lenders.

In this context, it was critically important for the U.S. Congress to show that it supported this mechanism by passing the quota legislation and by agreeing to the contribution to the IMF General Agreement to Borrow. In the rest of the world, there was much less difficulty. In fact, within a week of the U.S. legislation being passed, most of the rest had come in. The IMF has now obtained over 96 percent acceptance. While the immediate issue of the IMF quota increase has been resolved, there is a question of how the scale of its assistance should be increased. This issue was dormant while the quota legislation was in prospect.

I think it is unlikely that the IMF will be borrowing from the capital markets in order to increase the amount it can lend. It is clear that, in Congress and elsewhere, there are doubts about the degree to which public funds should be provided in this way and certainly a lot of emphasis on the need to have the commercial banks do the financing to the degree possible. This issue could well be reopened since, because of the imbalances mentioned, the countries needing the resources are suffering excessively. But at this point the imbalances are not likely to change very quickly.

Thus, the IMF is looking for ways to support other sources. The banks have been very cooperative in these critical cases by providing virtually complete rollover financing. There is not, in any of the key cases I have referred to, any net repayment on the outstanding principal. In addition, given the degree of difficulty of the situation, it was essential that the interest payments be covered at least partially by new lending. The package for Brazil included $6.5 billion from the banks to cover interest payments for a somewhat greater period than the calendar year—probably equivalent to about 60 percent of the interest that the banks would be receiving in that period—in order to moderate the cost of financing.

At the same time, some refinancing of the amounts that have been guaranteed by the export credit agencies or lent by official agencies is occurring through the Paris Club. That financing would provide another $2 billion or perhaps even $3 billion of resources to cover debt service. This is not quite comparable to the refinancing through the banks because the Paris Club amount does include refinancing of principal. The banks' $6.5 billion loan is in addition to a full rollover of principal. I should also mention that the banks have agreed to maintain outstanding short-term positions both on trade and interbank credits. These are also critical elements in avoiding undue pressure on Brazil's balance of payments.

The IMF tried, on top of that, to get a certain amount of official support. There has been agreement on $2.5 billion of additional export credit assistance. Eximbank would provide $1.5 billion, leaving about $1 billion for the rest of the world. Nevertheless, Brazil is going to have to work very hard, and the IMF in turn will have to ensure that the financing is, in fact, delivered.

Need for Trade Liberalization

I have mentioned the degree of adjustment underway in the major borrowing countries and the financing with which the IMF has been involved. There is also the critical question of future adjustment. Adjustment in that sense is not limited to the major borrowers' being obliged to live with a lower amount of capital; rather, it is a question of improving their export prospects and possibilities. It is very clear that, if the world is to function better or even to continue to function as well as it has, we have to give a new incentive and a new drive to the trading partners of the borrowing countries to buy their goods.

This, of course, is not primarily an IMF responsibility. The General Agreements on Tariff and Trade (GATT) was set up after the failed attempt to establish the International Trade Organization. The IMF has therefore been cooperating closely with the GATT to try to see what could be done. Mr. Dunkel, head of the GATT, has been meeting with IMG's managing director, every few weeks almost, to see whether the two groups can do anything jointly to make improvements in this area.

It is not difficult to see that these efforts do not appear at all likely to be rewarded by early action. The attempt at the GATT Ministerial Meeting ended virtually without substantial results. The United Nations Conference on Trade and Development (UNCTAD) in Belgrade, where trade issues were also featured, also ended without anything decisive taking place. Recent experience indicates that there is always easy acceptance of the general principles but that it is virtually impossible to obtain specific commitments, even on a standstill, to ensure that nothing will be done to restrict trade further. In addition, legislation on the books in the United States and other industrialized countries requires them to take certain restrictive actions under certain circumstances. Thus, it is not surprising that governments are unwilling to commit themselves further in the trade field.

The IMF and the GATT are struggling with the question of what can be done in this area. As Mr. Dunkel brought out at a meeting with the IMF, it is quite impossible for the finance ministers of the industrialized countries, meeting together as IMF members, to tell one of the major borrowers—Brazil, Mexico, the Philippines, or Korea—that they have to service their debt and work out ways to keep the financial system intact when the trade ministers of the same governments turn around and declare that they have difficulty accepting increased exports of steel or soybeans or other products. It is essential to recognize this inconsistency and to correct it. The financial arrangements that have proved so necessary and useful must be backed with actions on the trade front that will allow the borrowing countries to expand their exports. This backing requires, first and foremost, a clear recognition that it is self-destructive to aim at keeping jobs in the country if access to markets for foreign producers is choked off. In the absence of a viable system, the export industries of the advanced countries will suffer. Jobs that existed before will be lost, and the willingness of the Mexicos, Brazils, and Koreas to import will be eroded. It is a mutually destructive process. The example of the 1930s can be rightly cited as an analogy.

The IMF hopes, by being able to feature the logical impossibility in certain of these cases, to encourage, at least in a few specific cases—say, Brazil, Mexico, or Korea—the trade officials of partners to start to talk about the specifics of trade liberalization with the trade officials of these developing countries. To date, the response to IMF efforts has been uncertain, and the IMF has been encouraging some of the industrialized countries involved to indicate their willingness to deal with these issues. It is equally uncertain how willing the developing countries will be to start a process of negotiation, not knowing whether they will get anything out of it. It is awkward, but the shared impossibility of indefinitely continuing as before will lead to a willingness to start some marginal improvements. In this context, the IMF will do everything possible it can to back the GATT, if the initiative is taken up there, and to the extent needed, to initiate such discussions itself.

10
Consequences of the Austerity Policies in Latin America

Michael E. Curtin

The year 1981 was singular due to the cumulative impact of a series of economic developments and financial events which threw into doubt Latin America's ability to meet its international commitments and to continue its developmental growth. World trade value, which had increased at an annual rate of 20 percent through the 1970s, stagnated. Savings and investment, which had continued to grow despite several years of uncertainty, stagnated. Interest rates, reflecting the determined efforts of the industrialized nations to reduce inflation, rose to extraordinarily high levels—both nominally and in real terms.

The combination of trade and investment stagnation and high interest rates, coupled with an average price decline of principal export commodities of some 20 percent, and the convergence of maturities on its external debt in the short time frame converted Latin America's debt problem into a debt crisis. Had Latin America's exports continued to rise at a rate between 5 and 7 percent, the region would have had $35 billion more in 1982 and 1983. Had interest rates been two to three points lower, the region would have had an additional $10 billion. Forty-five billion dollars of foreign exchange during 1982 and 1983 would have made an enormous difference in the liquidity position—and thus the view of the crisis—in Latin America. This is not a denial of either the existence of a debt problem or the need for adjustments in the system but an attempt to find a long-range perspective from which to view the events.

The quadrupling of Latin America's external debt between 1973 and 1981 took place when there was a shared perception that the 6 percent average annual rate of real economic growth, experienced by the region since the early 1960s, would continue. We should not forget that over the 20 years from the 1960s to the 1980s, the GNP of Latin America tripled while that of the industrialized countries doubled; the average annual growth in industrial production had been about twice as large in Latin America as in the industrialized countries.

The absolute size of Latin America's debt today—roughly equivalent to one-half the regional product—may not be out of line with the long-term growth path of the regional economy. The current burden of debt service—roughly equivalent to one-half of the region's export earnings—may, however, hamper that growth, forestall the recovery, and prove to be a negative incentive to investment and savings. Thus, there is valid perception that the present liquidity crisis should not serve to shatter the prospects of future solvency.

Net external financing flows to the region underwent a dramatic change from the 1960s to the 1980s in terms of both amount and composition. It is important to understand these aspects of that change.

The annual amount of the net flow of resources, public and private, was less than $2 billion through 1965, averaged more than $4 billion during 1970 to 1972, jumped to more than $21 billion during 1978 to 1980, and peaked at $28 billion in 1981—a multiple of 15 times from 1960. The composition of the flow of resources has also changed dramatically. Official financing, multilateral and bilateral, declined from 60 percent of the total in 1961–1965, to 25 percent in 1971–1975, to 10 percent in 1977–1979, and recovered slightly to 16 percent in 1980–1981. Conversely, the flow of funds from the private commercial banking sector rose from less than 10 percent in the 1960s, to 42 percent in 1971–1975 and to 62 percent in 1977–1979. The other principal source, private direct investment, declined from roughly a third during the 1960s to a fifth during the late 1970s. It is a fact of economic reality that the consequence of the shift in composition of resources has been shorter terms and higher rates during a rising cost market for all providers of funds—both public and private.

The question in 1981 and 1982 was whether or not the Latin American countries would undertake the necessary, difficult, and painful adjustments needed to realign internal and external economic and financial variables. The answers to date are encouraging from a technical viewpoint. Three-fourths of the countries have negotiated programs with the IMF since Jamaica did in April 1981. Imports were cut by an average of 20 percent in 1982 and further in some cases in 1983. Public expenditures have been highly constrained or reduced. Foreign exchange rate measures, including some sizable devaluations, have taken place.

The effects to date have been dramatic from the human viewpoint. Consumption levels fell by close to 4 percent on a per capita basis. Both unemployment and underemployment have increased, to 30 percent in some countries and as high as 50 percent in some urban manufacturing and construction sectors. Per capita GDP, which has risen every year in constant dollars from 1960 to 1980, dropped in 1981 and more severely in 1982. In seven Latin American countries, the per capita GDP gains of a decade had been completely eliminated by the end of 1982; by the end of 1983, this number of countries will probably have doubled.

The impact of this retrogression is not uniform by country or by sector. It should be remembered that unemployment insurance and/or other welfare benefits are virtually nonexistent in Latin America. When one disaggregates the macroeconomic data to the personal human level, the impact in the burgeoning urban centers, where political power is now concentrated, cannot be overlooked or underestimated.

In terms of future consequences of national austerity programs on development, the first dimension to examine is overall investment levels. For Latin America as a whole, investment levels, measured in constant dollars, rose steadily through the 1970s, doubling from 1970 to 1980, rose 2 percent in 1981, then dropped by 13 percent in 1982. Investment levels, in 1980, fell in 6 countries and rose in 18; in 1981, they fell in 9 and rose in 15; in 1982, these levels fell in 17 while they were virtually stagnant in 5. In 1983, most likely, gross domestic investment fell in all 25 Latin American countries.

The companion dimension to examine is capital goods imports, which rose from $6.3 billion in 1971 to $37.4 billion in 1981, in nominal terms, which when adjusted for inflation is over a threefold increase in 10 years. The IDB estimates that OECD exports of capital goods to the region fell by over $8 billion, over 20 percent, during 1982. Projecting 1983 on first-half results of U.S. exports of capital goods, it may be expected that total OECD exports to the region will not exceed 50 percent of the 1981 level. In addition to the impact on Latin America, these figures have direct relevance in the OECD countries on exports, earnings, employment, and tax revenues. The IDB estimates that the reduction in capital goods exports translates to 400,000 fewer jobs in the OECD countries, principally in the United States.

While foregoing capital goods imports to meet contracted external obligations may serve short-term goals, when coupled with investment declines of the magnitudes being seen, it endangers the development of a structure capable of future economic growth and potential production for export to generate foreign exchange. While the short-term crisis has been averted by the willingness of the countries to implement adjustment policies and by their creditors, both public and private, to show flexibility in the face of new conditions, the IDB does not see that the structure of external indebtedness has been modified so that a reasonable balance between the willingness to sacrifice and the ability to sustain it has been reached.

During the months subsequent to the headlines in the press regarding the crisis in mid-1982, and even today, the principal focal point of the debate has been the short term. Much of the discussion in forums like this book has been on new institutions, new mechanisms, and alternatives for holding the system together, avoiding the unthinkable implications of default and disaster.

The fact that default has been avoided does not signal a return to normalcy. The fact that enormous sacrifices have been made, by all parties, does not mean they are sustainable over time. The fact that recovery may be attained through economic resurgence in the OECD countries, revived international trade, and lower global interest rates does not transform the structural problem. What about growth after recovery?

The squeeze on public expenditures that is going on and its inevitable interaction with private investment, coupled with the reduction of capital imports vital to future productivity, can be expected to result in either stagnation or moderately slow growth in the medium term after recovery. It does not appear likely that there can again be a period of explosive growth in international banking transactions comparable to that experienced during the 1970s. However, it does appear that continued and sustained participation by the private commercial banking sector, growing moderately with economic activity, is essential.

Private direct investment, both local and external, must increase, especially in the industrial sector, which accounts for almost 25 percent of the economic activity and approximately 20 percent of the employment in Latin America. Official financing, both bilateral and multilateral, must increase and be employed effectively and efficiently by those countries lacking present access to private markets and by those whose return to said markets will be restored over time. What then, is the Inter-American Development Bank (IDB) doing in this situation?

Negotiations were completed in 1983 among the bank's 43 member governments that proposed a substantial increase in its resources, so that from 1983 to 1986 the bank can have a lending program of about $13 billion in convertible currency. The board of governors determined at the same time the allocation of those resources by groups of countries, sectors of activity, and other relevant criteria. Therefore, the nature of the bank's lending program has already been established, and it corresponds to the priority areas of the region's long-term development.

The IDB has made certain adjustments to help its member countries cope with their critical immediate problems but without diverting its focus from the longer-term social and economic development objectives. The bank's approach is practical and rooted in its capabilities. For example, the bank is providing financing to help complete investment projects that are in danger of costly delays because of reduced counterpart capacity or reduced access to other external sources. The IDB is also providing financing—on a limited basis and for a limited period—to permit industrial reactivation where plant capacity for manufactured exports is underutilized because of foreign exchange constraints to purchase imported inputs. In some cases, accelerated disbursements of bank funds already committed in relation to when local contributions can be made—that is, modifying the mix—can make an important difference in early project completion.

The IDB is aware that in the total net flow of external resources to the region, the bank represents a relatively small portion. In the six or seven larger countries of Latin America that account for more than four-fifths of the region's external debt, the IDB's financial capacity cannot be, in the short run, a critical factor in the solution of the debt-servicing crisis. However, even for these countries, the bank is one of the few readily available sources of long-term lending on appropriate terms for development projects. IDB's financial contribution, again in terms of net flow, is significant for the intermediate-size countries and quite important for the small, least developed countries, where it often represents one-fourth or one-third and even more of the total. In the latter countries the bank does make a substantial difference—both in financial as well as developmental terms.

In conclusion, IDB believes that there are reasons for viewing the future of Latin America with optimism based on a realistic assessment of the accomplishments of the past. The undeniable facts that lead IDB to this optimism are the growth rates of close to 6 percent annually in real terms accomplished from 1960 to 1980, starting from the conditions that existed in the 1960s. This record, coupled with the productive investments made in both agriculture and industry, as well as in energy and physical infrastructure, has positioned the continent for future resumption of growth.

The realization and utilization of that potential, however, is critically dependent upon the availability of financial resources from both internal savings and the attraction of external resources. This availability in turn is dependent upon policies appropriate to growth and development as well as economic stability in the interdependent global framework. It is IDB's hope that in the near future, through meetings and dialogues, the focus of discussion and efforts of all concerned will once again turn to growth and development so that the crisis that has been averted does not recur.

11
Consequences of the National Austerity Program in Brazil

M.V. Pratini de Moraes

At the end of 1983, the Brazilian economy entered the fourth year in a row of the sternest program it has ever experienced since the Depression of the 1930s. This austerity program has brought about several changes in the economy. For instance, in 1983 Brazilian GNP was down by 6 percent, housing declined by 30 percent, and unemployment reached its highest peak relative to the total labor force (9 percent) in a country where 12 million are underemployed. Above all, the strictness of the program has revealed the basic commitment of the country to abide by the rules that have been negotiated with its international creditors. This chapter presents the current results of the austerity program and comments on the need to duplicate the measures already enforced by the other half of this interdependent program. Without a new commitment from the international financial community to enlarge capital flows to the debtor nations substantially, including Brazil, the strenuous effort undertaken thus far will only result in frustration and risks, both for Brazil and for the stability of the international financial system.

An evaluation of the stabilization program might reach the conclusion that results have been meager. In particular, if one considers that Brazil is enduring the most rigorous recession of the century, one wonders whether it has been worth carrying out the strategy pursued. Output per capita has declined more than 15 percent since the implementation of the austerity program in December 1980. Since the new letter of intent to the IMF calls for a further deceleration in monetary growth, very few analysts now predict a positive result for output growth in 1984.

There are scarcely any doubts that part of the problem was caused by domestic policies. Monetary and fiscal policies were highly expansionary in 1979 and early 1980, prompting the need for a drastic change in policy at the end of that period. To aggravate matters, the resulting overvaluation of the cruzeiro, a consequence of the ceiling placed on the accumulated devaluation in 1980, turned the current account deficit worse and brought forth the austerity measures.

It is important, however, to call attention to the fact that the international economic situation was not conducive to adjustment in 1979 and 1980. The new round of oil price hikes deprived Brazil of much-needed foreign exchange balances during a stage when they were severely needed. The fall in the terms of trade also aggravated matters. If one takes 1977 as the basis for comparison, Brazilian terms of trade declined steadily over the period up to 1982 when the accumulated fall amounted to more than 50 percent.

This drastic deterioration in terms of trade made worse a problem that was already serious enough. Measured in terms of foreign exchange cash flow, the real interest rate faced by Brazil in the international market skyrocketed. If one takes the developing countries' export-price deflators to arrive at the relevant real interest rate on international loans, one will come to the amazing figure of 20 percent by 1982. Of course, this real interest rate burden stemmed both from the violent jump in nominal rates and the decline in terms of trade referred to earlier. In any case, the need to assure continuity to induce capital flows into the economy compelled the authorities in Brazil to align the internal real interest rates with the international real rates, thus provoking the decline of real output per capita.

The violent increase in real interest rates in the international market also implied serious and perverse effects on the balance of payments. On the one hand, high international interest rates negatively affected growth prospects for the industrialized nations. The ensuing recession and unemployment had an impact directly on Brazilian exports, both through a decline in the rate of growth of demand and through increased protectionism. By the same token, the jump in nominal rates increased interest payments to a point beyond the ability of the economy to generate the necessary cash flow in foreign exchange. Expenditures on interest, which in 1978 amounted to a little over U.S.$3 billion, jumped to U.S.$5.4 billion in 1979, to U.S.$7.5 billion in 1980, to U.S.$10.3 billion in 1981, and to U.S.$12.6 billion in 1982. As a result, the services account deficit tripled in a period of 5 years. It is significant to point out that the services deficit, which accounted for 39 percent of total exports in 1978, increased steadily until 1982 when it reached 77 percent.

It is also worthwhile to recall that in Latin America the problem with foreign debt is magnified by the large concentration of that debt in the banking system. For the area as a whole, some two-thirds of the debt is owed to the banks. This concentration has had adverse consequences for countries like Brazil since the changing moods of the international banks particularly affect the financing of the debt service. The large growth of short-term debt after 1980 has contributed to uncertainty about the financing of the current account deficit. This lack of assurance became even more evident after the decision of the banking system to reduce exposure in the developing countries, particularly in Latin America.

The austerity program in Brazil began in May 1980 when the government initiated a stabilization program similar to those that were agreed upon with the IMF. However, there were no rigid targets for the reduction of the public deficits. In 1980, the exchange rate policy was also not as firm as it is now. The program comprised a process of monetary adjustment based on three basic instruments.

The first was a reduction in real wages by adjusting salaries at rates below that of inflation. The second was a drastic reduction in the real liquidity of the economy. Between May 1980 and September 1983, the monetary base was reduced by 53 percent in real terms. The real liquidity, M1, was reduced by 64 percent, and the real liquidity in relation to gross internal product is 70 percent lower in 1972. If you consider liquidity including M1 plus the short-term Treasury bonds, it was at the end of 1983 48 percent lower than in 1972. At the same time, inflation increased substantially, indicating an increase in the velocity of money.

The third basic instrument of this policy was to increase taxes. Brazil increased personal income tax, corporate income tax, and all taxes on financial income. At the end of 1983, it also increased the sales tax, which is a state tax, and substantially increased the tax on cigarettes. In addition, Brazil substantially reduced and almost eliminated all subsidies, especially on wheat and bread, use of liquefied petroleum gas for cooking, and all agricultural and export credits to reduce the public deficit.

There is scarcely any doubt that the austerity program enacted in Brazil—and in almost all of the Latin American countries—can work only if capital flows are maintained at certain levels. To assure the continuation of these capital flows, many domestic measures have been undertaken. Real interest rates domestically are now as high as 30 percent, and inflation has skyrocketed in response to major devaluations enacted both to avoid capital flights and to increase export competitiveness. Truly, one cannot disregard the fact that the Brazilian inflation rate, which ran in 1983 around 200 percent, owes a lot to the forced maxi-devaluation of the cruzeiro in February 1982.

Brazil's economic policy, however, has yielded impressive results as far as the external accounts are concerned. The current account deficit has declined in 1983 to slightly over U.S.$7.5 billion, after reaching U.S.$11 billion and U.S.$14.8 billion respectively in 1981 and 1982. Export growth, which suffered very much from the world recession, has recovered due to improved competitiveness and was growing at an annual seasonally adjusted rate of 7 percent in the last quarter of 1983. This was due in part to the effects of the devaluation and maintenance of an accelerated crawling peg, as well as measures aimed at restricting growth in domestic nominal wages. Import control has also played a major role. In 1983 imports declined some 25 percent relative to the already depressed levels of 1982. In fact, measured by a quantity index, imports are back at the levels prevailing in 1974. This helps to explain why per capital output declined so much in such a short period of time and reinforces the argument offered earlier that despite the meager effects, the program enacted has been particularly tough.

However, there are some good signs. Agriculture production is increasing, and in 1983, in spite of all the difficulties, it was increased by more than 3 percent. Brazil expects in 1984 an additional increase in the agriculture crop area. For soybeans the increase was 10 percent and for corn, 12 percent. This is good music for Brazilian people, but it is bad music for its competitors.

In 1983, Brazil became the world's second largest exporter of raw steel, Japan being the first. Steel and steel manufacturers today represent the most important export of Brazil, more than coffee, iron ore, and soybeans. Twenty percent of Brazil's exports in 1984 will be of steel and steel products.

In 1983, for the first time, steel was produced in Brazil more cheaply than in Japan. The latest figures show that two of the Brazilian steel companies produced steel more cheaply than both Kawasaki and Nippon Steel in terms of industrial costs, of course, not in terms of financial costs.

Brazil is becoming a leading exporter of aluminum. It is building two of the world's largest aluminum smelters in the Amazon basin and a third in Rio de Janeiro. Brazil is also becoming a leading exporter of pulp and paper. In 1984 more than 50 percent of all its energy needs were supplied by hydroelectricity and some coal-burning thermal centers.

The basic question now refers to the availability of capital flows over the next couple of years. New bank loans to the developing countries have declined markedly since 1982. According to estimates made by Pedro Pablo Kuczynski in chapter 8, the net flow over the second half of 1982 totaled only U.S.$5 billion, compared with a U.S.$25 billion annual rate from 1979 through the first half of 1982. Needless to say, the sudden interruption of capital flows requires, from the debtor countries, adjustment beyond their physical capabilities. The problem is compounded by the retrenchment of new trade financing, by both the banks and official export agencies. Since most of the developing countries are now facing severe domestic recessions, lack of trade financing imposes an additional burden to countries, like Brazil, that used to export a significant share of their manufactured exports to the developing world.

Economists have great expectations that the industrialized nations will soon be growing at the magic figure of 3 percent and that interest rates will remain at current levels. They also hope that the price of oil will remain stable in real terms or even decline slightly. Last, but not least, they trust that trade barriers will be reduced as the recovery gathers momentum, thus imparting an expressive inducement to increase exports from the developing countries to the industrialized world. The problem is that fulfillment of these conditions is not enough. It takes time for the recovery to gather momentum, for protectionism to be reduced following reduction in unemployment, and for real rates of interest to fall. There is a pressing need to do something in the intervening period to solve the liquidity problems of the debtor countries.

Brazil has done its part. Its austerity program has been the most rigorous enacted in this centruy. These policy measures have been undertaken as the country adjusted itself to reap the benefits of returning to full democratic institutions. It is undisputed that, were it not for Congress's support to the stabilization program, it would be almost inconceivable to have the measures enacted without major social unrest. The gradual return to democracy is playing a vital role in this context, a role that will be enhanced in the future.

By the same token, Brazil has continued to abide by the decision to honor its international obligations, however difficult the domestic consequences might be. This is a long-standing pledge. But unilateral commitments are not enough to secure a lasting way to steer the country out of the international liquidity crisis. While no one contends that the main responsibility now rests with the international banks, investors, and governments of the industrialized nations to play their part in this interdependent program, the coming years will tell whether Brazil's sacrifice was a sound contribution to world financial stability or a waste of a wealth so persistently acquired with much hardship.

12
Consequences of the National Austerity Program in Mexico

Angel Gurria

The LDCs now have large fiscal and external deficits. They are running high levels of inflation, and almost all have debt problems. These factors make adjustment necessary. Adjustment, of course, is an elegant synonym of low growth, no growth, or negative growth, and it is deemed necessary to tackle the debt crisis.

If there is no adjustment, there will be deficits, inflation, and worse debt problems. One thing more that will happen is that these effects will be accompanied by total disorder and eventually by a very severe curtailment of net new flows, either of foreign investment or of the spontaneous market flows that are indispensable over the long term. That is why adjustment is necessary.

There are essentially only two ways to go. One is adjustment and the other is financing. Whether there is financing or adjustment, the end solution is going to depend on the proportions that a country has of these two. There is nothing else, nothing in the middle or on the sides.

The mix between adjustment and financing is directly related to the availability of financing and the possibility of adjustment, and these will be different for each country. Clearly in the past, even in the recent past, there was almost unlimited availability of financing. Therefore, there was very little adjustment. Now there seem to be too many demands for adjustment, and very little financing is available.

That particular balance is the one Mexico has to redress. The right balance between adjustment and financing is crucial, and this is mostly what the debt negotiations have been about. Basically, the answer to the question of whether adjustment is needed is yes. Is it crucial? Yes. Does Mexico have to let adjustment choke it? Obviously not. The country has to combine adjustment with some degree of financing, some level of financing that is consistent with a minimum of welfare. Let me emphasize that I am indicating a minimum for everything. Mexico is no longer shooting for the stars—only for minima that are consistent with keeping its societies mostly how they are today. They are probably poorer than they should be, but no one wants to see them fall apart. If Mexico does not strike the right balance between adjustment and financing and the minima are not achieved, minimum welfare will change, and it will change for the worse—for the worse for Mexico and for the industrialized countries too.

For 30 years Mexico's GNP grew at about 6 percent. From 1978 to 1981 it grew at 8 percent. However, adjustment means that in 1982 it grew at −0.2 percent, basically 0. In 1983 Mexico's GNP grew at −3.5 percent and Mexico hopes in 1984 to start growing at 1 percent. That is adjustment, after 30 years, almost 40 years of unmitigated and continuous aggressive growth. In 1982, all countries in Latin America, with the exception of Trinidad and Tobago, grew negatively in terms of per capita income. 1983 was the same.

Mexicans are now looking at 1983 and 1984 as years in which not only will the country not grow but also the standards of living will fall for the first time in 40 years. Seventy-five to 80 percent of Mexico's population is below the age of 30, and therefore, a lot of these people have only known economic growth.

It is said that arithmetically the only solution to the problem of few resources is that you must get more and spend less, which is a very obvious arithmetic solution. All countries are striving to get more resources. They are all raising the prices of services and goods that are sold by the public sector. They are all increasing taxes and trying to raise public revenue.

For example, in Mexico gasoline was selling at 6 pesos per liter in August 1982. At the end of 1983 it was 30 pesos per liter, and Mexico is an oil-producing country. The same is happening to electricity. Mexico raised the value of the electricity tax from 10 to 15 percent because raising the income tax is not going to produce any income in a falling economy. Mexico is raising the price of everything it can lay its hands on. In fact, Mexico is even freeing some of the controlled private sector prices to encourage production and basically also to encourage tax revenues at the same time as an indirect impact.

Mexico is also reducing expenditure very dramatically. The way to reduce expenditure is measured as a deficit of the percentage of GDP. The country exaggerated in the past. It got to 18 percent in 1982 and was brought down to 8.5 percent in 1983 and to 5.5 percent in 1984. It was very painful for Mexico to bring the deficit down from 18 to 8.5 percent. But it is going to be almost as painful to bring it down from 8.5 to 5.5 percent because the fat is gone.

What has happened to real wages? In all the formulas for adjustment, real wages have to fall. In Mexico's case, they have fallen about 30 percent from 1982 to 1983. In 1984 they did not fall any further because

Mexico is running a country, not a social experiment. It does not want to find where the limits are but to stay a bit short of the limits. However, real wages fell 30 percent only in one year. That shows how difficult and painful these adjustments can be.

In 1984 there will not be further erosion, but there will not be any catching up either. Mexico will not encourage the recuperation of lost purchasing power, which means the purchasing power of the people will still remain vis-à-vis 1982, very depressed, 25 to 30 percent lower. When compared to 1981, where the country was hit with 100 percent inflation and was not expecting it, the figure is even more than 30 percent.

Adjustment requires a balance of payments compression; the foreign sector has to be adjusted. What has this adjustment meant for Mexico? In 1981 it imported $24 billion of merchandise. Imports fell to $14 billion in 1982 and dropped further to $9 billion in 1983. Mexico hopes to catch up a bit and go to $14 billion in 1984.

The Mexican current account deficit was $13 billion in 1981 and fell to $3 billion in 1982. It ran a surplus in 1983 of $3.5 billion in the current account. In 1984 the country will run a small deficit of about $1 billion. From a $13.5 billion deficit to a $3.5 billion surplus in two years: that is adjustment.

Interest rates in Mexico used to be negative vis-à-vis inflation. In most of the Latin American countries it was the same. Mexico had an interest rate of 40 percent with an inflation rate of 80 percent. In August 1983, the interest rate was 60 percent with an inflation rate of about 70 percent. But if you multiply the yield, because the interest was paid monthly, the real rate was barely positive. Now inflation is coming down a bit: Nominal rates are still 55 percent, and real rates are positive.

Savings are increasing, but what does that do to investment? It does not help much, but in this case one has to be extremely careful about the mix. If the real rates are too high, there will be disincentive for investment. The exchange rate was 25 to 1 in January 1982. At the end of 1983 it was 150 to 1—that is foreign exchange realism. It is realism because Mexico made these decisions after a long period of waiting. However, it is hard on the inflation figures and on individual companies that have dollar debt. On balance, it is good to have a realistic exchange rate, but when a country has to move very fast, it is very traumatic.

In terms of the debt restructuring, all the countries in Latin America, except maybe Colombia or Tinidad, and many others in the rest of the world are restructuring. Restructuring is extremely expensive. Mexico pays the full rate, 6 percent in real terms against 3 percent in the past, and that over a long period of time. It has been indicated that the debt-servicing costs to Latin America are around $10 billion a year.

The debt problem has also been politicized. It has caused tremendous problems in Brazil and in Argentina. The governor of the Central Bank of Argentina was put in jail because of it. In Venezuela, it clearly was a main campaign issue in the elections of December 1983.

The debt problem is not only a problem of payment capacity. While a country is restructuring its debt, there is no medium-term framework. People are not certain about the country: the nationals and banks are uncertain about the future. This uncertainty is not taken into consideration. Banks think a country can go on restructuring every year. But Mexico cannot because it needs a medium-term framework and a minimum of assurance of what is going to happen in the future.

For countries it is very expensive and politically very inconvenient to be running a constantly unstable financial scenario because it spills over into politics. Most important, however, adjustments are about people. Every one of the figures I have mentioned has hit the people very hard. If countries and their governments are pushed too hard when they have to choose between the banks and their external creditors and their people, they will always choose for the people. It might be a short-term decision, but they will choose for the people. If they are pushed too hard, if the environment continues to be hostile, then there will be a further deterioration of the situation.

The muddling-through scenario is the only scenario that I see for the future; I see no breakthroughs. Mexico needs too many things—for example, growth and the IMF, the World Bank, and the IDB. Mexico needs governments to lend money to the developing countries. It needs aid that is presently very inadequate. It needs lower interest rates. It needs bank loans, continued commercial bank lending, and trade liberalization. These needs will not be met all together, and some of them might not be met at all.

The debtor countries should not be lumped together with only one ruler to measure them. The tape measure for how much of an adjustment program a particular country can take depends on the particular country. The IMF is beginning to take this into consideration. But even in the case of Mexico, which so far is a success story that has shown very good results, when Mexican representatives go to Washington, they always feel like spendthrifts, that the country is throwing money away and doing everything wrong. The IMF always makes Mexicans feel that they have come for a report card. The Mexicans expect to get a pat on the back, and the IMF says, "Well, that's about as much as we thought you'd do, but how about next year?" However, the representatives say, "Wait, this year is not over."

Adjustment is dramatic, and it has been happening in Mexico for the last 2 years, at least, and will continue to happen, in some cases under a controlled scenario. A concerted and organized approach to each Latin American country continues to be critical lest countries continue to fail to reach their goals and choose a political solution, the short way out, the easy way out, the politically easy way out that is not toward discipline, not control, but toward false doors, basically demagogic exits, and that way out can make the international financial system very unstable indeed.

13
Adjusting to the Economic Recession: The African Experience

Herbert M. Onitiri

In an age in which we care so much about human rights and human values, an assessment of the impact of economic recessions must go beyond their effects on prices, output, and incomes and dwell ultimately on how they affect human beings and the economic and social conditions in which they live and work. Within that framework, the economic recession of 1980 to 1983 has had a far more profound impact on the developing countries than it has had on developed societies. This should not come as a surprise. While in many developed societies the institutional framework for relieving unemployment and for promoting social security, basic health, and other services did not completely insulate the population from the impact of the recession, it certainly provided a safety net to minimize the human suffering and deprivation that would have resulted from the recession. In developing societies, particularly the poorer ones where such institutional safeguards hardly exist, the impact of the recession has to be evaluated in terms of countless millions of people subjected to hunger, deprivations, and destitution as well as the loss of production capacity owing to the shortage of foreign exchange for importing parts, components, and the vital equipment that are needed to maintain existing infrastructures.

Within the group of developing countries, the African countries have suffered the worst impact of the recession because their economic structures are not sufficiently responsive to changes in international demand and prices. In the first place, after 20 years of political independence, many African countries are still dangerously dependent on a narrow range of primary commodity exports, and these are precisely the commodities that have been most affected by the recession. According to the World Bank Development Report, 1983, after adjusting for the rise in prices of manufactures imported by developing countries, real commodity prices in U.S. dollars were lower in 1982 than at any time since World War II. In addition, domestic industries in many African countries are still at such a rudimentary level that they cannot provide substitutes for many of the imported items that are vital to domestic development. Thus, at times of critical foreign exchange shortages, expensive capital equipment lies idle because the country cannot afford to pay even for little items such as nuts and bolts, to say nothing of more expensive components and raw materials. Finally, the linkages between imports, exports, and the domestic economy are still so tenuous that when export demand falls, there is little possibility of shifting domestic resources from export production into production for home use. Products such as coffee, cocoa, bauxite, and iron ore rely almost entirely on the vagaries of foreign markets.

What has made the African situation particularly serious is that many of the countries are still struggling to adjust to the effect of the increase in oil prices while in the midst of recession. Partly because of borrowing to meet the higher costs of energy supplies, the external debt of Sub-Saharan African countries, excluding the four oil exporters, rose from $4.4 billion in 1970 to $26.26 billion in 1979. The situation got worse in subsequent years as a result of the recession. Between 1980 and 1982, for example, the total debt of developing Africa rose by about 14 percent.

The inflow of financial resources, and the consequent rise in foreign indebtedness, did not prevent a steady decline in the rate of growth of the GDP during the 1970s and up to 1982. According to the World Bank Development Report, 1983, the average annual percentage growth of the GDP from 1960 to 1973 was 3.5. In 1973 to 1979, it fell to 1.5 percent, while the figures for 1980, 1981, and 1982 were respectively 1.2, 0.1, and 0.8 percent. Assuming an average annual growth of population of 2.5 percent, the GDP figures would imply a steady decline in GDP per capita since 1973.

The seriousness of the African situation has touched off a major debate about causes and possible solutions. In fact, there has been very little controversy about the long-term effects of inherited colonial structures and what the World Bank has described as the "economic disruption that accompanied decolonialization and postcolonial consolidation." There has also been little doubt about the destabilizing effects of external factors such as higher energy prices, economic recession, slow growth of primary commodity trade, and adverse terms of trade. Furthermore, a consensus seems to have emerged on the need to increase substantially overall resource transfers to African countries and to improve the terms of transfers during the next 10 years, while at the same time promoting measures to increase the productivity of investment through better management and more efficient reordering of development priorities.

The real controversial issues have centered on the question Have these factors been eased or been made worse by domestic policies in the

African countries? In particular, critics have asked whether or not too much of a role has been given to government and too little to private enterprise, whether or not government controls and regulations have been overused in preference to market forces, whether or not rural development has been put at a disadvantage compared with urban development, and whether or not too much emphasis has been put on building high-cost, heavily protected domestic industries to the detriment of agricultural development and export promotion.

It is certainly not my intention here to continue what has not always been a very constructive debate. However, a very important question is How can the impact of external fluctuations on the weaker economies be minimized? It would be helpful if developed countries would use methods to stabilize their economies other than periodic recourse to deflationary and inflationary policies. But as long as external markets are subject to unexpected fluctuations, African countries must prepare to adjust to the impact of these fluctuations on the domestic economies. The real lesson of the current recession is that, given the present scope of interdependence in the world economy, recession is too costly a method for bringing down inflation and that the cost, in human terms, tends to be particularly high for low-income developing countries.

Take, for example, the issue of export promotion versus import substitution. One argument is that African policies are biased against exports and that more foreign exchange could be earned by promoting exports and diverting resources from import substitution. The examples of South Korea, Taiwan, Singapore, and Hong Kong are often cited in this connection. This statement is not completely devoid of truth. The countries cited have certainly made impressive showings in the export markets of the industrial countries, and I believe that African countries should also join this group to the extent possible and produce labor-intensive manufactures for the markets of developed economies. This statement of course assumes that markets will remain open in developed countries and that the present pressures for protective policies will be contained.

African countries have to learn two lessons from the experience of these newly industrializing countries. The first is the importance of maintaining a high level of productivity in a highly competitive world, and the second is the need to adopt a domestic income policy that keeps a tight rein on domestic income in relation to the level of domestic output. While changes in the exchange rate can be important, these can do more harm than good without effective policies on domestic productivity and income.

How much each country will be able to adopt such policies will depend on a complex of political and social forces, quite apart from economic considerations. However, assuming that some countries are able to set themselves on the appropriate courses of action, they are still likely to run into critical obstacles and bottlenecks that may mean the difference between success and failure. The fact of the matter is that many of the African countries are suffering from major deficiencies in critical economic and social infrastructures that will have to be considerably alleviated if measures for productivity improvement and income policies are to succeed. This is exactly what the Brandt Commission had in mind when it proposed a special program of action for the poverty belts of Africa and Asia. It will be recalled that the commission had said in its report, *North-South—A Programme for Survival*, that:

> An action programme must be launched comprising emergency and longer-term measures, to assist the poverty belts of Africa and Asia and particularly the least developed countries. Measures would include large regional projects of water and soil management; the provision of health care and the eradication of such diseases as river-blindness, malaria, sleeping sickness and bilharzia; afforestation projects; solar energy development; mineral and petroleum exploration; and support for industrialization, transport and other infrastructural investment.

For many African countries, such an action program is indispensable to the creation of productive and flexible economic structures that will be more responsive to market signals and increase the capabilities of the economies to withstand the impact of external shocks. Since this kind of program cannot be promoted by the ordinary rules of foreign investment, the task of the international community is to ensure that the flow of resources to the poorest African countries contains a large element of concessional assistance.

There is another kind of program that I believe would be crucial for future economic stability in the African countries. This program involves the stability of primary commodity markets, on which very little progress has been made in recent years. The opposition to the stabilization of primary commodity markets on the ground of noninterference with market forces has always sounded rather hollow in the face of extensive control and regulation of the markets for many agricultural commodities in the developed economies. Although such controls and regulations have been subjected to frequent debate and discussion, there is no reason to expect that the Common Agricultural Policy of the European Economic Community (EEC) or the agricultural support policies of other developed countries will be replaced in the foreseeable future by the free interplay of supply and demand. It is time to be a little more realistic on this matter and to give more support to the UNCTAD Common Fund and the conclusion of individual commodity agreements without which the fund cannot be fully effective.

What the poorest African countries require to get them out of the present impasse is a package of measures involving more concessional assistance, more investment, and a number of critical reforms of domestic policies. In fact, many African countries have already embarked on difficult, painful, and often politically sensitive reforms of domestic policies. This is acknowledged in the report by the World Bank, *Sub-Saharan Africa: Progress Report on Development Prospects and Programs*, which noted, "It would be an international tragedy if, at a time when the willingness of African governments to rethink and revise their programs was increasing, donors in general and contributors to IDA [International Development Association] in particular could not mobilize commensurate financial support for these countries."

14
External Financial Inflows in Non-Oil-Exporting African Countries: Problems and Prospects

S.A. Ogunleye

International finance and trade are subjects of particular interest to the African Development Bank (ADB) not only because it is closely involved in that field for the African region but also because the functioning, or one might say malfunctioning, of the international financial and trading system has become increasingly conspicuous in its effects even on people living in remote areas in rural Africa. This chapter gives an African perspective on the current problems of international finance and trade—in particular, on the subject of external financial inflows in African countries—and suggests broad policy directions—both international and domestic in character—that might ease the ongoing economic crisis in the 1980s and beyond.

Non-oil-developing Africa's terms of trade, which had improved over the period from 1973 to 1978, fell drastically by an estimated total of 17 percent in the period from 1978 to 1982. Export volume growth was very sluggish after 1979 and declined absolutely in 1981, while export prices fell substantially in both 1981 and 1982. These developments led to a steep drop in the import purchasing power of exports of more than 12 percent over 1979 to 1983. As a consequence of the resulting foreign exchange shortage, the volume of imports stagnated in 1980 and declined in both 1981 and 1982. Despite the policy-induced restrictions on imports, however, the current account deficit (excluding official transfers) widened considerably from about U.S.$9.5 billion in 1978 to an average of nearly U.S.$14 billion from 1981 to 1983. Over the same period, the cover of international financial reserves dropped from over 6 weeks of imports to only 3 weeks.

The persistent deterioration in the external account has, among other effects, adversely influenced further export expansion in a number of countries and has contributed to higher inflation and fiscal imbalances. The import restraint, which has resulted from the reduced import capacity, has led to transport and export-processing bottlenecks that have thus reduced export expansion. Inadequate availability of imported industrial raw materials and spare parts has led to lower-capacity utilization in industry and therefore to higher average costs and prices and to lower sales tax revenues. Since the latter is a large element of government recurrent revenues, fiscal balance has been negatively affected.

Part of policy reaction to the rapidly deteriorating external and domestic situations has been increased foreign borrowing. The external debt for the non-oil-exporting African region is estimated to have risen from U.S.$42 billion in 1978 to about U.S$75 billion in 1983. This was during a period when the cost of borrowing was rising rapidly. The external debt-servicing payments as a proportion of exports of goods and services rose from 12 percent in 1978 to exceed 20 percent in 1982. The contribution of interest payments in this ratio increased from below 5 percent to nearly 9 percent. Current payments arrears accumulated, while a number of countries in the region were forced to renegotiate their multilateral loans.

From the figures of the external accounts cited, it will be seen that non-oil-exporting African countries have faced a serious financing problem in the past 4 years or so. Net official external transfer inflows almost stagnated in nominal terms between 1979 and 1983 and must therefore have substantially declined in real terms. Other net capital inflows declined in nominal terms between 1980 and 1982, and despite the expected moderate recovery in 1983, also showed a drop in volume terms over the whole period from 1980 to 1983. This serious external financing problem is likely to persist in the medium term as total official development assistance, on which Africa heavily depends for capital account financing, will probably show no growth under present policies in the major industrial countries. With respect to commercial borrowing, African countries—like many other developing countries—are more constrained in their borrowing choices because of the changes in the volume, structure, and particularly in the terms of their debt since the mid-1970s. Further constraints—in the near term at least—are high real interest rates and depressed prospects for their exports. The latter implies low debt-servicing capacity and therefore low creditworthiness for many countries of the region. Given the medium-term international economic outlook, serious efforts by African countries to borrow on private markets—even assuming that would succeed—would indeed lead to severe debt problems.

A major point that should be stressed is the well-recognized fact of economic interdependence among nations. This fact has been well documented and argued in the Brandt Commission Report and its later followup documents, in the recently published Commonwealth Study Group Report entitled *Towards a New Bretton Woods*, and in many other documents. It is therefore unnecessary to repeat the theories and statistics. Despite the wide recognition of interdependence, however, macroeconomic policies in the major countries continue to be conducted largely within a national economy framework, paying little attention to the wider macroeconomic implications of their actions. As has been painfully demonstrated by the deep recession of the early 1980s, uncoordinated and narrow economic policies can be costly to everyone. Such policies are particularly adverse to the poor nations where sharp deceleration or decline in economic growth condemns large numbers of people to absolute poverty. Economic interdependence therefore should guide the conduct of macroeconomic policies in both the major and small countries if the 1980s are to provide any hope of further human advancement.

There is every danger that domestic national policies in Africa could increasingly turn toward economic retrenchment and deflation to avoid further financial deterioration and, one might say, bankruptcy. Such a policy stance would clearly be against global recovery and would fall hard on key public services aimed at eliminating absolute poverty. In a more constructive light, however, the situation calls for serious domestic policy tightening aimed at promoting growth and external balance in wide-ranging areas such as the development of more appropriate domestic pricing policies; the improvement of institutions, particularly those servicing the agricultural sector; and the increased efficiency of resource use in both the private and public sectors.

In the current tight situation, however, the ADB has to agree with the World Bank's *Sub-Saharan Africa Progress Report,* published in September 1983, that increased external assistance is critical to the domestic policy reform efforts:

> The early stages of policy reform which are being implemented in many countries need to be nurtured, while in several other countries, governments are likely to be observing what level of external support they can expect if they embark on major programmes of policy reform. This need for increased external support is reinforced by the dramatic fall in primary commodity prices since 1980. Attempts by African governments to implement policy reforms which will improve their balance of payments situation and prospects are being frustrated by deteriorated terms of trade.

These words capture very well the interrelationship between the domestic policy efforts and international financial flows for facing the current crisis in Africa and, in the context of interdependence already stressed, for global recovery.

The interrelationship between domestic policy or growth on the one hand and international finance and trade on the other can be stated even more precisely. The desirable relationship is one that ensures a stable and expanding capacity to import on the part of the African or developing countries generally and that therefore supports economic growth, demand, and global prosperity. In suggesting such a desirable relationship, one must admit, of course, that it can only function smoothly if appropriate policies that support economic expansion and demand are in place in the major industrialized countries. Reasonable economic expansion in the industrialized countries, for instance, would support higher prices and volumes of developing country exports and therefore improve the latter's import capacity. Increased economic interdependence means that economic activity in the various countries would tend to rise and fall together.

For that reason the ADB suggests that underlying all major reforms in the world financial and trading system must be efforts not only to promote policy coordination especially in the major countries but also to expand effective participation in key international institutions by Third World countries. The tendency has been to treat financial issues—for example, in the IMF, World Bank, and regional development banks—separately from trade issues—for example, in GATT and UNCTAD—giving marginal attention to related matters. A combined forum is certainly an idea to be recommended.

The issue of stabilizing and expanding developing country import capacity and therefore total financial inflows can be separated between efforts aimed at stabilizing and increasing export proceeds on the one hand and of enhancing medium- and long-term capital flows on the other. With respect to the stabilization and enhancement of export proceeds, the issues revolve first around the support of buoyant export demand that comes through adequate aggregate demand expansion, the rolling back of protectionist measures, and other associated policies in the industrialized countries. Second, the issues revolve around commodity price stabilization measures that have been internationally suggested through arrangements like UNCTAD's Integrated Programme for Commodities, including the establishment of a Common Fund to finance international commodity agreements and related arrangements for individual commodities. However, despite the agreement in 1980 to establish the Common Fund, subsequent achievements have been very limited. Moreover, the agreed size and functions of the Common Fund are much smaller than those originally envisaged.

Closely associated with these efforts are the desirable reforms in the IMF's compensatory financing of export shortfalls. Although well established, the Compensatory Financing Facility (CFF) has provided inadequate funding vis-à-vis actual export falls. Greater stabilization of developing country import capacity could come via reforms that tie CFF financing more closely to exogenously induced shortfalls rather than to country quotas, that take into consideration general import prices, and that extend repayment periods to allow greater ability to repay. It should be stressed that the outlook for the 1980s points to a very great need to increase Africa's import capacity via commodity price and other stabilization measures. It is projected, for instance, that for 11 major export commodities of Sub-Saharan Africa (excluding oil), which from 1976 to 1978 constituted over 50 percent of all exports, the export price index in the 1980s will be 15 to 20 percent below the prices prevailing in the 1960s or the level obtained in the second half of the 1970s.

The inflows of medium- and long-term capital to finance African development is of particular importance given the relatively high dependence of the region for capital account financing and the declines in volume terms already described. The interrelationship of such capital with domestic growth-oriented policy reforms has also been stressed. Given the income levels of the majority of African countries, concessionary Official Development Assistance (ODA) assumes a more pronounced role that is heightened by the very inadequate provisions made for low-income countries in existing mechanisms for expanding international liquidity and the failure to stabilize commodity prices and earnings.

Despite the international declarations on the role of ODA, however, the OECD members' ODA remains on average only 0.39 of GNP, in comparison with the 0.7 percent United Nations target for the 1970s. But the need by African countries for external financing has been amply demonstrated in the figures quoted earlier. Africa's hope, therefore, is that the donor countries that have not reached the target will take seriously the pledges made at UNCTAD VI to increase their efforts, while those that have not written off their debts to the poorer countries will quickly do so. Furthermore, given the compression of imports already indicated by earlier statistics on Africa, it is highly desirable that an increased share of financial assistance be given for program rather than project financing to allow greater flexibility and availability of operational imports.

Related to program financing is the need for expanding the resources of multilateral institutions including those of regional development banks. These institutions are better placed to assess country programs and policies and therefore to assist balanced economic expansion. The ADB Group highly welcomes the equity participation by nonregional countries and is already doing some work toward program lending. At a different level, however, the bank remains disappointed by the difficulties facing soft-window financing, particularly with regard to the IDA replenishments in the World Bank Group and the African Development Fund of the ADB group.

Finally, medium- and long-term capital inflows in Africa can be increased through the encouragement of foreign private capital. Although the role of such capital remains small in general, the potential could be sizable, particularly if domestic policy is conducive to it. Foreign private investment has the advantage of sharing in investment risk and bringing with it skills and technology and is therefore beneficial if appropriate codes of conduct, particularly on the activities of transnational corporations, can be established. The regional development banks like the ADB as well as the IMF and the lenders and investors of individual countries should give greater consideration to this matter in Africa.

Part V
Consequences of Changing World Trade and Investment Patterns and Policies: A Case Study of Steel

15
The State of the World Steel Industry

William T. Hogan, S.J.

The steel industry today on a worldwide basis is in a depressed and difficult position. This has been true in the United States for the past 3 years and has been true in Western Europe for many more years. In fact, since the steel boom of 1973 and 1974 when world records were established, the industry in Europe has had difficult times.

If we look at the profit and loss statements of the companies, we find that losses in the last 6 years have been astronomical as hundreds of millions of dollars have been lost by individual companies. In 1983 in France, Usinor and Sacilor, the two main divisions of the nationalized French steel industry, lost about $1 billion, which is about 4 percent of the personal income tax collected by the French government. The same is true of many other companies around the world. These financial losses have caused the companies to rethink their plans for the future.

In the early 1970s, the industry was in a state of euphoria. There had been continual growth from the end of World War II through 1974 hardly without a letup. Plans were for more and more steel capacity to be installed throughout the world in Europe, in Japan, in the United States, and in Third World countries. In fact, in 1974, we might estimate that on a worldwide basis, excluding the Soviet sphere, 240 million tons of capacity would be added between 1974 and 1985. With the depression that hit Europe in 1975 and subsequently the United States and Japan, and a declining world market for steel, these plans had to be reassessed.

As a result of this reassessment, the steel companies, instead of planning for expansion, are planning for contraction. They are cutting back the amount of steel capacity in most of the industrialized countries in the world.

The French, for example, have reduced their capacity by several million tons, and it appears that they may reduce a little bit more. The British Steel Corporation has reduced its capacity from 28 million tons, when it was first organized in 1967 and the industry was nationalized, to over 14 million tons in 1982. The Germans are in a state of confusion today.

Mergers were recommended for the major companies, and these have fallen through. Nevertheless, the Germans will reduce their capacity by 3 to 4 million tons. The Belgians are in the same position, and Arbed in Luxembourg is looking to reduce capacity by ridding itself of a couple of plants that were acquired in Germany.

Thus, we see that Western Europe will have a smaller industry in the future, and this is important because a smaller industry will mean that obsolete and high-cost facilities will be abandoned and that the industry will be operating with a much higher proportion of competitive, modern equipment.

Examining Japan, we find that the Japanese built an industry in the 1960s to serve not only the Japanese market but also the world market. They saw a growing world market and built a very large industry, twice as large as they need for their domestic market. Consequently, the Japanese depend on exports to survive.

The Japanese have the most modern, largest industry in the world, built completely after World War II, most of it in the 1960s and early 1970s. They now find, however, due to growth of the Third World steel industry, that they have a smaller share of the world market and must reduce operations.

Japan has a nominal capacity to produce about 150 million metric tons of raw steel. However, true capacity is probably about 135 million tons. In 1983, a little less than 100 million tons were produced, which represented about 66 percent of their nominal capacity and some 73 percent of their actual capacity. In 1984, projected output is approximately 103 million tons, which is significantly below the 1973 record of 119 million tons.

The Japanese have a problem when it comes to reducing steel-making capacity since their political and social structure does not allow them to abandon plants in the manner in which it is done in the United States. When the Japanese close a facility, they try to provide jobs for as many of their people as possible to the point of transferring them long distances to another plant. For most of the last few years, one-third of their blast furnaces have been closed down, and it is relatively certain that a number of these will never be restarted.

The Western European outlook for the future is quite pessimistic. Most of the steel companies feel that there is very little growth left for steel use throughout Europe. They point to the automotive industry where demand is now somewhat saturated. In place of one car for every 10 to 15 people, which was the case in the early 1960s, most Western Europeans have one car for every 3 to 4 people. Thus, they figure that the market is saturated in respect to its growth potential, leaving mainly a replacement market. Further, they feel the capital goods market in Europe is also a replacement market with very little growth anticipated. Western European participation in Third World steel markets has been dwindling because the Third World is installing capacity of its own and because of considerable competition from the Japanese and others.

In terms of outlook, the Japanese are not quite as pessimistic as the Europeans. They see a strong possibility for growth in China although in other areas growth will decline. The industry in Japan is continuing to modernize and update its plants so it can provide a quality product at a low cost in order to compete in the world market. If the Japanese do not export 25 million tons of steel, they are in trouble (in the past exports have been as high as 37 million tons although the average in recent years was closer to 30 million tons).

In the United States, there is also a decline in the size of the steel industry. In 1983, capacity was listed at approximately 150 million net tons. In early 1984, this was revised downward to 135 million net tons and will be further reduced to less than 130 million net tons by 1985.

There are no plans among the major producers for any expansion; indeed, the opposite is true as a number of integrated companies are closing plants and combining facilities. Total reduction will be some 20 million tons in facilities having obsolete, high-cost equipment for the most part so that the U.S. industry, when it is finished restructuring, will be operating fewer but more productive plants. Presently, any investment made by the U.S. steel companies is directed toward modernizing equipment by installing facilities like continuous casting and reducing costs, particularly in relation to energy. Continuous casting eliminates some traditional steps in the production cycle and also provides a better product.

With the reduction in capacity, the question has been raised as to whether the U.S. industry will be capable of serving its domestic market. To answer this, one must examine not only the supply of steel but also the demand for it. Further, it must be recognized that the demand for steel is a derived demand. It comes from the demand for the products of steel-consuming industries, and the steel industry can do nothing to stimulate this demand. If the public is not buying cars, steel sales to the automotive industry will be considerably reduced. The same is true of the capital goods segment of the economy. If investment in plant and equipment is down, steel sales will react accordingly. This is one reason why the steel industry in the United States has not participated in the recovery. The U.S. recovery has been centered in the consumer durable goods market rather than in new plant and equipment. The capital goods segment of the economy admittedly is the last to experience a recovery, and when and if this happens, they hope during 1984, it will have a favorable impact on the steel industry in the United States.

The automobile industry in the United States has experienced a sharp, permanent decline in terms of steel consumption. This is due to the reduction in the size of automobiles so that currently an average of 1.1 tons of steel are necessary per car produced as compared to 2 tons in 1973. Further, imports have taken a substantial portion of the market so that the tonnage shipped to the automobile industry will be approximately 10 million tons below the peak shipments of the 1970s. The same is true of containers. Since aluminum and plastics have taken a significant portion of the market, about 3 million tons have been permanently lost to steel. Thus, even with a reduced capacity, the steel industry in the United States will be able to satisfy at least 85, possibly 90, percent of the domestic requirements.

Throughout the industrialized world, the steel industry is shrinking, yet what remains will be a better industry with more modern and more competitive facilities. This is fortunate since the industry on a worldwide basis will operate at a higher rate of capacity and will be able to compete within its own limits, as well as with other materials such as aluminum, plastics, and concrete.

Unlike the industrialized world, steel companies in the Third World are anxious to grow. Between 1975 and 1980, when industrialized world steel operations declined sharply, output in the Third World increased by over 60 percent. Some countries had a most spectacular growth in the 1970s and early 1980s. For example, in 1971, South Korea produced approximately 500,000 tons of steel, and in 1983, output was almost 12 million tons. The South Koreans have what is probably the most modern plant in the world since it was the last one built. It is a large plant capable of producing over 9 million tons of raw steel and operates with low costs since employment costs are about $3 an hour compared to more than $20 in the United States, $13 in Japan, and from $14 to $16 in Western Europe.

South Korea is planning to build an additional plant that is the only new grass-roots steel plant under consideration in the world. In terms of investment, the South Koreans are going to be able to construct the plant at a very reasonable cost since every steel mill manufacturer and equipment producer is looking to sell to South Korea. They hope to construct the plant for $800 a ton of installed capacity, which compares with an estimated $1,500 or even $2,000 per ton in other places.

Taiwan is also adding more capacity. Brazil brought on a new plant in November 1983 with 3 million tons of steel-making capacity, all of which will be confined to semifinished steel. An additional plant will be put in operation late in 1984 or early 1985 with 2 million tons of capacity.

Thus, although steel capacity is shrinking in the industrialized world, it is expanding modestly in the Third World. The world currently has too much capacity for the current rate of demand. However, with the shrinkage of capacity that is taking place and a moderate recovery in demand, there should be better times in the steel industry in the latter part of the 1980s.

In conclusion, I shall provide some observations on steel trade restrictions. The quota system established with the EEC steel producers, as well as the voluntary restraint imposed by the Japanese on themselves, were calculated to reduce steel imports into the United States. However, in 1983, imports increased a small amount over the 1982 figure. The steel companies were fully aware of this fact since the numbers were posted month by month. A substantial increase came from the steel producers of the Third World. The fact that suits involving antidumping and countervailing duties were not submitted immediately is based on the need to prepare such a case so that it can be defended when filed. Further, once the case is filed, it normally takes 300 days before the procedures that lead to relief are completed. Thus, with the preparation and filing of such suits, an 18-month period can be required. This is unfortunate because a considerable amount of damage can be done in this period before there is any redress. Cases were being prepared in 1983 against a number of countries and have since been submitted.

It takes time to prepare these cases, and it costs money. Small companies are not able to make such an investment, so it is up to the large companies to shoulder the burden. In some instances, the U.S. Commerce Department has taken the initiative. It would be good, however, if a procedure could be devised to allow these suits to be prepared and adjudicated more rapidly.

Another point that should be stressed when the term *protectionism* is used, and I think it would be better to use *defense*, is that the United States is not the only country that has instituted means of protecting its steel industry. The EEC has both quotas and price restrictions. Japan is now importing 3 to 4 percent of its steel requirements, and the industry there is clamoring for some sort of protection against imports. They now want to protect themselves against Korean imports. A number of countries in the Third World have very strict protection devices. For example, in some Latin American countries, the steel companies do the importing and sell the product. Thus, I think we should recognize that it is not the United States against the world in terms of protection.

Most countries protect their steel industries to avoid unemployment, which is high on the list of problems, particularly in Europe. Many of the European governments would rather subsidize a company that is losing money to keep people working than have them unemployed and on the dole. This, in itself, is not a bad idea, but once products are exported at prices below the cost of production, problems are created in countries where the steel industry is not government owned or subsidized and is forced to make ends meet in order to survive.

As for the future, there is no problem that a 15 to 20 percent increase in the demand for steel will not cure. In 1973 and 1974, there were no trade problems. The steel industries of the world were booming. No one thought about restraining imports; in fact, the demand for steel was so great that end users were willing to pay high prices to obtain it. U.S. trade problems will be solved with an increase in steel demand that will bring about a much higher rate of operations, particularly since the industry on a worldwide basis will shrink in size over the next few years.

16
Problems of the U.S. Steel Industry

Joseph Spetrini

The U.S. steel industry is operating at about 59 percent of capacity at a time when its industrial economy is supposedly recovering. Total U.S. manufacturing capacity utilization is running at around 78 percent, whereas total industrial manufacturing capability utilization is running around 78.5 percent. Thus, the steel industry is running about 20 percent less than that, which is not out of line in terms of the way a normal recovery proceeds. However, it is taking a long time to get the expected results from an economic recovery. At the same time, the United States is suffering from very depressed prices from all sources. The fact that a sector of the world steel industry is growing is really complicating the situation. It has grave implications for public policy questions and to what extent an open trading system for steel is maintained in the United States.

It is a difficult and emotional issue, and it is a tough economic nut to crack. There are a host of opinions, and most of them are hotly contested. The issue is becoming more emotional as the United States continues to have something in the order of 97,000 unemployed steelworkers.

The development of steel production capability by Third World countries has contributed to this excess capacity. Between 1973 and 1982 raw steel production capability in the Third World doubled to 82 million tons. In 1982 these countries accounted for about 17 percent of worldwide production capabilities.

This increase in production capability resulted basically from development policies that stressed the importance of a national steel industry for further industrial development, further employment, and the earning of foreign exchange. However, subsidies and other forms of assistance were often provided to encourage this development, and this, of course, is something of a problem from the point of view of U.S. trade laws.

In the mid-1970s, when many of the decisions to invest in steel capacity were made, steel production in the Third World countries was less than half of their total consumption, a balance that has changed considerably. Moreover, domestic consumption in the Third World countries was expected to soar as the hoped-for industrialization was to take place.

Unfortunately, the oil crisis contributed to recessions. High debt burdens slowed the rate of growth in these newly developing countries. Thus, the result has been reduced domestic demand for steel, excess domestic capacity, and a greater than expected propensity to export. In addition, Third World countries burdened with a high level of debt have looked to steel exports as a means of earning desperately needed foreign exchange often to pay for the steel mills as well as other domestic burdens.

The strong dollar has made already attractively priced imports from these Third World countries even more attractive in the U.S. market and again has resulted in a marked increase in Third World production. The United States is particularly concerned about the continued investment in steel capacity by some Third World countries. This investment clearly is not needed for domestic consumption. It merely exacerbates the problems of overcapacity and depressed prices.

The United States realizes the pressing need for foreign exchange for these countries but fails to see how the growth of an industry in a market characterized by persistent excess capacity, reduced demand, and depressed prices is of benefit to anyone. At the same time, worldwide production capability has increased. The demand for steel has declined due to both cyclical and structural factors.

Between 1979 and 1981, steel consumption in the Western world decreased by almost 6 percent. Global economic recession accounted for only a part of this decline because a lot of it was due to structural change. In terms of the long-term prospects for steel demand, the United States has factors like quality improvements that result in stronger, lighter, more durable steel. It also has aluminum, cement, and plastics substituting progressively for more steel consumption. Also, changes in the end product, like lighter, smaller cars, have reduced the demand for steel in the United States and in the other countries.

While these changes were occurring, the U.S. industry was incurring an increasingly higher cost, resulting in a diminished ability to modernize plant equipment and production facilities, and thereby problems from competitors were compounded by the inability in some cases to keep up.

Some of the decrease in demand is temporary. Already demand in some product lines has picked up in the United States as a result of the economic recovery. For example, while the operating rate for the U.S. industry as a whole was only 59.3 percent during the week ending 3 December 1983, mills making products like sheet steel used in the automotive and appliance industries were operating at much higher levels. Shipments of sheet products rose from 2 million net tons in December 1982, the nadir of the past recession, to 3.2 million net tons in September

1983, an increase of 55 percent. When we think of this large increase, that 59.3 percent operating rate becomes even more dramatic. Structurals and plates and some of the other products tied to the capital goods sector are really extremely depressed, operating in the 30 or 40 percent range.

The fundamental changes in this international supply, demand, and competitiveness around the world have contributed to the present situation in which 97,000 U.S. steelworkers, about 28 percent of the steel work force, are on layoff and almost all of the major U.S. producers report losses in their steel operations. These changes are also reflected in trade statistics. Imports from countries other than the European community producers, Japan and Canada, during the first 9 months of 1983 were 44 percent above the same period in 1981 and 1982. Imports were at about 3 million tons for the first 9 months of 1981 and 1982. Most of the imports from these countries are now subject to some form of trade action by the U.S. government, such as antidumping, contravening duty investigation, or suspension agreements as an alternative to investigations resulting from either alleged or confirmed unfair trade practices.

While recovery has bitten some parts of the industry, it is very narrow and very fragile though it is relieving some of the immediate problems of depressed demand. The U.S. industry still must adjust to the structural changes in international supply and demand through the rationalization and modernization of the existing production facilities. In the past 6 years, U.S. production capability has dropped 10 percent. Investment in plants and technologies is being made. However, these investments are seriously limited by the financial losses plaguing the industry. For example, the efficient process of continuous casting, which only accounted for 9.1 percent of steel produced in the United States in 1975, accounted for about 27 percent of production in 1982, and it rose to nearly 31 percent in 1983. Again, this is partly a result of the fact that a lot of the non-continuous-cast capacity had to be cut back because the prices were not attractive enough to produce it or there just was not enough demand.

A labor union has also recognized the fact that something has to be done. For the first time the United Steelworkers contract negotiated in March 1983 involved wage and benefit cutbacks. That was something unheard of in this country and, of course, is part of the problem. But the fact that the workers appreciate this and have attempted in their own way to contribute to this situation is encouraging.

The proposed merger of two major U.S. steel companies that is now under consideration by the Justice Department is another possible addition to the rationalization process. Some analysts expect that this merger, if it is approved by the Justice Department, will allow these companies to take advantage of each other's efficient plants and eliminate some of their redundant capacity.

Other countries are also in the process of adjusting to the dramatic changes in the world steel sector. The European communities are in the midst of a difficult restructuring effort that is aimed at reducing capacity by over 25 million metric tons and limiting government subsidies by the end of 1985.

Japanese steel firms, considered among the world's most efficient producers, are also feeling the need to adjust to changes. Last year for the first time steel output in Japan fell below 100 million tons, and imports have captured a record 10 percent of the Japanese market, something that was unheard of only a short time ago. Of course, a lot of this import business came from South Korea, and the Japanese can thank themselves for helping the Koreans build very efficient steel mills, which seems to be a common problem these days. Japanese steel companies are now talking about diversifying into nonsteel engineering materials such as ceramics, carbon, fiber, coal, chemicals, and superalloys.

The U.S. government has taken a number of steps to attempt, from a public policy point of view, to contribute to the improvement of the current situation. Recently it has instituted changes in tax laws to enable steel and steel-consuming industries among others to accelerate the depreciation of equipment and facilities. The metric volume compliance regulations for the U.S. steel industry have been modified to allow for more cost-effective methods of complying with the law. The Commerce and Labor Departments have announced the formation of a steel advisory committee that will permit government management and labor representatives to discuss and evaluate alternatives for addressing the industry's long-term problems.

In conjunction with these measures, the administration has vigorously enforced U.S. trade laws. In order to make the varying types of economies mesh, each country has to enforce its own laws that have to be consistent with the GATT, whether it is a subsidy code or the antidumping code. People who engage in international price discrimination or subsidization as a means to maintain uneconomic capacity artificially are not helping. Such moves will wash back into their markets and hurt everyone.

The economists can tell you that problems do not go away by sending them to other countries; they will return in one form or another. Basically, the United States wants to ensure that unimpeded fair trade is allowed to enable development in the U.S. economy and the economies of the trading partners. However, countries ambitious to grow industrially and in the broader sense need to appreciate that certain of these practices are not helpful. And this problem is going to continue to be an emotional and very difficult economic problem until some improvement is made in beggar-thy-neighbor policies.

17
Armco: A Case Study

Robert E. Boni

As Armco's president and chief operating officer, I represent a variety, maybe eight or ten, of constituencies. In this chapter I only address this problem as it relates to three of these constituencies: Armco's employees, lenders, and shareholders.

Armco announced in 1982 that it is closing down its Houston, Texas, steel plant. That steel plant at one time employed 5,000 people; more recently it has employed 1,100. The plant provided steel plates, structurals, and bars to the energy industry and a variety of other industries. Being located on the Houston ship channel, it was specially vulnerable to imports of steel from countries like Brazil, Rumania, and Poland.

Armco had to close the plant down because it was losing about $4 to $5 million a month. The reason for this loss was the need to compete with steel that was imported at costs or prices lower than those for which Armco could produce the steel. It is that simple. Prices eroded and then volume eroded as the energy markets declined. Thus, the company was confronted with the classic problem of not having enough market, and the market that existed was at too low a price for it to stay in business.

From the lenders' and the shareholders' points of view, this close down is very costly. The losses and the writedown of the equity of the Houston works cost about $230 million dollars—a loss of almost $4 per share in terms of the book value of Armco. Lenders did not look very kindly toward that event, and they downgraded Armco's long-term bond rating. As a result, if Armco is to borrow money from those sources in the future, it will cost more money.

However, let me illustrate how a close down affects an individual employee. One of my basic concerns is what happens to employees of my company, Armco, and what is happening to them is no different than what is happening to steel employees within many of the steel companies throughout the developed nations. Following is a description of a real person. His name is Joe Washington. Joe had been with Armco for quite a number of years and is a very good machinist. He is a widower who is 46 years old. Joe has a son in high school, and he has about 11 years left on the mortgage of his home. He has one car, and the family was relying on what Joe could earn as a steel employee in the Houston, Texas, plant.

Joe's plant closed, and along with it, his job, and this is just one consequence of the changing world pattern in steel. I knew Joe and liked him, and I have a great aching in my heart for a great number of employees like Joe all over the world. I can hear their voices when they worry about whether they can pay their mortgages and whether or not they can make a living. The effect of the lost jobs on Joe Washington and the rest of those employees in Houston, Texas, alone is going to cost the city several hundred million dollars in revenues. Everybody suffers—the individual and the community. Armco is having to undergo some massive retraining programs in Houston for the employees that were involved, and that same thing is happening all over the United States.

Now the discussion turns to a region that is not in the United States. Being on a major river, this region is served by cheap water transportation, which is an economic element of a good steel company. It has rail and highway networks and sits in the midst of a huge industrial area. The other thing a steel company needs is a market. The region makes automobiles, machinery, equipment, appliances, and a multitude of construction products. It has relatively cheap energy—another element required for an economic steel company. It also has a superbly trained and highly motivated work force—an essential.

This particular area has a history of technological innovation. Another important factor is to have a good technological base and to be receptive to technological change. Well, that particular area I am talking about brings about iron ore and coal and turns out a variety of finished steel products.

Now, the steel maker in this area is working at around 50 to 60 percent of capacity utilization. Thirteen percent of its people have lost their jobs. The companies in that region of the world have lost a great deal of money, and people are leaving the area. Some politicians in the region are trying to explain the loss in terms of whether it is a structural or a cyclical problem. I am not describing the Ohio Valley but the Ruhr Valley. Thus we see that what is happening in the United States is happening also in the EEC. If conditions continue, it will happen in Japan as well.

The Ruhr, Liverpool, Charleroi, and Kobi areas face the same sort of tragedy as in the Ohio Valley of the United States and in Houston, Texas. The world's greatest and most efficient steel-making enterprises are being disrupted, not just the inefficient high-cost steel producers.

I think about 270,000 jobs in the steel-working area have disappeared in the United States, and we cannot ignore the fact that there is a great deal of excess capacity in the world today. I would estimate that today there is about 200 million tons of excess steel capacity in the world.

The United States, recognizing that the steel industry has to change, is trying to buy some time for necessary modernization. At the same time, some restraint is beginning to appear in imports from the EEC and Japan, with a corresponding lack of restraint in the LDCs. That is one of the difficulties today. We continue to rationalize at Armco, as does Bethlehem Steel, and we see a merger of J & L and Republic as well as possibly other mergers in the United States. But we are not seeing the same kind of restraint in the developing countries. There is an announcement, for example, of a new Brazilian company, of Korean expansion, as well as expansion throughout the rest of the world.

What the United States is asking for is restraint. The country is faced with a four-part dilemma. First, clearly there is an uneconomic Third World steel capacity in place and more expansion under way. Second, this surplus capacity is being operated at extremely and unrealistically high rates of capacity utilization. Third, these countries' internal economies have no foreseeable way in the future of using this steel. Thus, immense tonnages of that steel are being exported to the United States. Fourth, the United States, being one of the finest markets for consumption of steel, is a primary target.

Much of the U.S. capacity should be rationalized and terminated. However, it is meaningless for the United States and the EEC to rationalize and for Japan, at last, to be thinking sensibly about reducing its capacity if there is continuing expansion that is subsidized in the rest of the world. Steel is not unfairly traded. It is illegally traded because it violates certain laws.

If the current question is how Third World debts are to be repaid, the answer is that there will have to be compromises. A single industry cannot be expected to bear the full brunt of such a problem. Over $300 billion of that debt is in countries that have growing steel industries, and they intend to pay off those loans partly by shipping steel into the United States.

The steel industry has proposed a law, called HR 4352, which we call the Fair Trade in Steel Act of 1983. All the industry is asking for is a quota of 15 percent. That represents a cutback from about 19.6 percent of apparent domestic capacity that is imported. Passing that rule will enable the U.S. industry to become more competitive over a period of 5 years. The door will still be open to imports. The steel industry is not saying erect barriers, but it is saying enough is enough.

18
Steel Trade Restrictions:
A Critical View

Robert M. Gottschalk

I do not think anyone can be for or against any issue in trade without being concerned as to its impact, not only in his or her country but also in other countries. However, before analyzing how U.S. legislation is affecting trade, we have to keep in mind that Americans are on both sides of the issue. Whenever you restrict the import of a product, you may disfavor the industry manufacturing that product. You will disfavor Americans on the other side who are importing it, further finishing it, or in some fashion are involved perhaps in transporting it.

Thus, we have to be terribly careful when we speak of trade legislation that suddenly puts a 15 percent quota on imports of foreign steel as if it is self-evident that this is in the best interests of the United States. The legislation will affect enterprises across the United States from the dock to the ultimate consumer. While we must be sympathetic toward the unemployed steelworkers, we must realize there are workers on the other side of the fence whose dependence on steel at a reasonable price may not be favored by the legislation. The following sections discuss some of the terms of this legislation.

Dumping

Dumping is injury found from the sale of a product at so-called less than fair value. In very broad terms, *less than fair value* means sold in the United States for less than the average sales price in the home market.

It is clear also that if in the home market all of the sales are made below the cost of production and the U.S. sales are even less, there is a problem, and at that point there is a method of calculating the cost of production. It is ethical, legal, moral, and virtuous to sell below fair value. The only time it becomes subject to an additional duty, which is deductible from taxes as an expense, is in the event it is found to cause injury.

Dumping is not immoral. It is done every day in a range of products by all countries. It only becomes subject to an additional duty under certain circumstances.

Countervailing Duty

Certain subsidies given by any government to an industry within its borders may under certain circumstances be deemed to be countervailable, meaning those subsidies may be deemed to be of such a nature as to allow the country to which the product is exported to add a duty because of the subsidy. Again, does it make it illegal, immoral, or anything else to give subsidies? The answer is no because there are certain consequences that may flow from this act.

It is important to remember that any application of trade laws that is consistent with GATT is not protectionist. Perhaps I am defining it narrowly, but if members have agreed to the measures that can be applied, it seems illogical to consider those who apply them to be immoral or improper. The word *protectionism* is a pejorative term.

The ignorance of bankers in the trade area is legendary. It may even be increasing. Bankers are very good at their tasks and have learned to use political risk analysis. They can evaluate when the government of Nigeria will change before the State Department can. However, when it comes to trade risk analysis, bankers are not so good. They will lend money to a company to manufacture a product, the destination of which may be closed by the time the factory is completed. They do not exert the same degree of concern for the practicalities of trade restrictions that they do for the fall of a government. However, there are more trade restrictions than falls of governments, and there are more factors that will affect products than the fall of a king or of a prime minister. The lesson is that the banks cannot maintain this level of ignorance much longer.

An administration economist recently recommended that large amounts of funds be made available to the developing countries to enable them to finance the construction of new projects. These countries would in turn export their products to hard currency countries like the United States, thereby receiving the money necessary to repay their debts. It is a superb scenario with one major flaw: When the product arrives in the United States, it will be hit with countervailing duties because it has been subsidized with funds that originally came from the United States. That is the case with Brazilian steel and will be repeated with a number of other products.

Domestic legislation is not replaced by agreements like the Caribbean Basin initiative. Under that initiative, a number of islands will be assisted in industrializing, but their products will never come into the United States because it will bar them at the border with the existing legislation, which is not going away. Bankers, being in the first line of lending for the construction of this world, ought to know what is happening to their money and what risks they are taking with it and should know more about trade than they do now.

Are there issues, are there remedies, are there things that can be done? My objection to the U.S. steel industry is not their having brought antidumping or countervailing duty complaints but their using those complaints as a blackmail weapon to obtain something else. This industry has on four occasions used attacks to get relief that is not meant to be given under the trade laws. The first time, it was the first trigger price, a price-fixing mechanism about as much in violation of U.S. precepts as any. The second time, it was another trigger price mechanism. The third time involved an arrangement limiting imports with the EEC. The fourth instance was a case filed in December 1983 by Bethlehem Steel, putting in question all imports of steel into the United States and aiming at a worldwide limitation on imports. This is not what the trade legislation was intended to do.

If bankers had reacted earlier, they might have prevented the subtle use of power that is being exercised now by the U.S. steel industry. What can the banks do about it? Knowledge goes a long way. Learn sensitivity to risks as they develop, monitoring of trade pattern changes, and early reaction. If the banks do this, do it carefully, then there is a chance of having a sane world in which to operate.

19

The Dilemma Faced by the Steel Industry in the Developing Countries: The Brazilian Example

M.V. Pratini de Moraes

This chapter explains the factors behind the Brazilian steel expansion. In 1970 I was in the United States and had a meeting at the Eximbank. Henry Kerns was the chairman. He told me he would give me a blank check for the Brazilian expansion program in the steel industry. Those were the headlines in *The New York Times*. I went to the World Bank and was promised $300 million to make steel in Brazil.

Then I went to the IDB, and they promised at least $200 million. I then went to the United Kingdom, and they said they would finance everything I need. Then I went to Germany. I was received by Dr. Szold, the chairman of Thyssen. He said, "Marcus, we take care of *alles*. So anything you buy from Germany, anything you buy from us, Dresdner, Commerzbank, or Deutschebank, *keine problem*."

I went to Japan where I saw the prime minister and the minister of international trade. They said the Eximbank would give me $60 million to start. They ended up financing $400 million. The conditions were 12 years at a 6 percent fixed rate. In Belgium, they said, "We will finance anything you buy from here," and we bought electrical equipment.

The objective at that time was to expand Brazilian steel production from 4 million tons to 20 million tons of capacity. The idea was to operate at an average of 90 percent, producing 18 million tons, of which 16 to 17 million were to be used in the internal market and 1 to 2 million tons exported, to be taken by Kawasake Steel. This was done.

What were the reasons for such investment? First, Brazil has a large internal market. Second, Brazil has the biggest iron ore reserves in the world. Its iron ore has the highest content of iron—usually, 65 to 67 percent of iron content. In Europe it is some 35 or 40 percent iron content. The geography of steel production inevitably had to change.

But other things have changed too. The price of oil increased, thus increasing transportation costs. When Brazil went to the markets to export, it faced difficulties because it was exporting more than had been planned due to the internal recession.

Brazil is criticized because it gives subsidies. All countries give subsidies, including the United States. Some countries are more open about it than others. In the case of Japan it is very difficult to find exactly how subsidies are given; but they do it and they do it well. European companies give lots of subsidies, especially through their official banks and export credits. Brazil gives no subsidies. The simple thing is this: the developing countries, and Brazil especially, traditionally have had an overvalued currency. All primary-goods-exporting countries for centuries have had overvalued currencies. When Brazil began to industrialize, industry began to press for more protectionism in terms of exchange rates. Only very recently in Brazil has the cruzeiro come close to its true value.

What are export subsidies? Export subsidies in Brazil, as in most developing nations, are a means to adjust overvalued exchange rates to the national currency. Brazil is so competitive in the areas of coffee, cocoa, and other primary goods that it has to tax exports of these products by as much as 50 percent to avoid a tremendous increase in income to the producer of these products. As exchange rates go up and as the value of the cruzeiro, for instance, gets closer to its real worth, subsidies are immediately eliminated, and most of them have, in fact, been eliminated during the last couple of years.

I shall now make an additional comment on the question of jobs and the damage done to industrialized countries. There is a big problem in the traditional industries of countries whether to maintain old jobs or to create new jobs. It is a problem even in Brazil. Because of the structure of trade between Brazil and the United States, imports from the United States to Brazil create many more jobs than exports from Brazil to the United States endanger employment in the U.S. exports.

This may not be true with the trade between other countries and the United States or even with the trade between Brazil and Europe. However, there is no doubt that for every dollar of exports that Brazil sells to the United States, it imports at least $1 and probably more than $1. This is not happening right now since Brazil has to have a substantial trade surplus because of the bankers. Thus, the country is in a difficult position. The bankers tell Brazil to run a huge trade surplus, and it tries to do it. Brazil goes to the United States, where they tell Brazil that it subsidizes exports. It is a difficult situation, but it is not a problem without solution.

There is a very strong economic justification to produce in Brazil because there is no doubt it can produce pulp and paper, aluminum, steel, and a number of other products more cheaply than any other country in the world. This is not due to lower labor costs but because, as in the case of paper and pulp, the trees grown for pulp need only 6 years to be used in the pulp industry. In Sweden they need 30 or 40 years. In the case of iron ore, Brazil has the world's largest reserves. U.S. steel was for a long time involved in iron ore in Brazil, and most international steel companies have some kind of joint venture there. They have, for instance, palletizing plants. There are 14 palletized projects in Brazil, of which 8 or 9 are in production in association with foreign steel companies.

In the case of aluminum, Alcoa, Alcan, the Japanese companies, and even Italian companies are also involved in producing bauxite, alumina, and aluminum in Brazil. Brazil has lower steel production costs than Japan. Thus, I think there is economic sense in these projects not only because the costs of production can be low but also because the internal market can justify large projects or large investments.

During 1984, maybe next year, for the short run there will be some difficulty in using this production internally and in exporting because of restricted markets. But what I would like the bankers to evaluate is that the more Brazil can export, the faster the bankers will be repayed. It is a simple fact of life that if Brazil gets earnings from exports, the speed with which foreign debts and interests can be paid is, of course, increased. Brazil would like to have the bankers on its side now that it wants to export, the same way they were on Brazil's side when it imported the machines to produce the steel and all these other products.

Part VI
The Future: Prospects for Refinancing and Trade Expansion in the 1980s

20
The International Debt Problem: Working Out a Solution

R.T. McNamar

I n September 1982, the international financial community was virtually paralyzed with fear. Mexico, Brazil, Argentina, and Yugoslavia appeared to be on the brink of economic collapse. The mood at the Annual Meeting of the IMF and World Bank in Toronto was almost universally morose. Fear was widespread that the world's banking system would collapse, bringing an implosion of trade and inevitable worldwide depression.

At the end of 1983 things were quite different. The 1983 IMF Annual Meeting was upbeat, positive, and forward looking. Financial flows had been at least temporarily restored. And developing countries from Mexico to Asia were adopting and implementing policies that would make them, once again, strong members of the Free World's trading and financial systems.

I now explore the events that have brought us to the threshold of a new phase in the international debt problem, the third and final phase, that should lead to an eventual resolution of the situation. However, to comprehend fully the implications of this new phase, we must understand Phases I and II.

Origins of the Problem

The LDC debt problem was created by the global economic environment of the 1970s. First, rapid oil price increases drained financial resources from the LDCs into the hands of a few OPEC members. A study by the Institute for International Economics traces $260 billion of LDC debt—53 percent of the total increase in non-oil-exporting LDC debt between 1973 and 1982—directly to the OPEC oil price increases. In addition, in the creditor countries, high inflation, even high commodity prices, and negative real interest rates—that is, interest rates below the level of inflation—distorted the world's economy, and inflationary expectations for the future became the norm for the world's policymakers and private citizens. Under these conditions, the buildup of developing country debt is understandable.

From the LDCs' point of view, borrowing appeared to make sense because creditor countries' inflation rates often exceeded the interest rates on the loans. In such an environment, virtually any increase in debt is rational because by the next year, while interest costs will have added to the level of debt, inflation will have increased the nominal value of exports even more. Debt burdens, even if onerous at first, could be counted on through inflation to ease over time. Indeed, Brazil, Korea, and the Philippines borrowed externally to build indigenous energy capacity to decrease their sharply higher oil bills. Accordingly, many LDCs tended to seek as much additional debt as the lenders would provide.

From the bankers' perspective, the buildup of debt was also understandable. Between 1974 and 1981, OPEC's cumulative current account surplus totaled some $386 billion. Lacking adequate internal investment opportunities, these countries placed excess funds in the world's major banks. The banks found that the borrowers most willing to pay for loans were the newly industrializing developing countries. In addition, banks could point to healthy future prospects for many LDCs such as Mexico with its vast oil reserves and Brazil, whose exports grew tenfold between 1969 and 1981.

Conventional wisdom was that high inflation and negative real interest rates and even higher oil prices would continue. The Blue Chip Economic Forecast in November 1980 foresaw U.S. inflation rising from its average of 7.3 percent in the second half of the 1970s to 8.9 percent for the period between 1981 and 1985. Real interest rates were predicted to rise by only 3/4 of 1 percent over the negative levels experienced in the late 1970s. In short, too many people assumed the environment would not change. However, while the developing countries and bankers acted rationally on the whole, they also made mistakes.

Many developing countries chose to avoid adjusting economic policies and to accept temporary reductions in living standards caused by the drain of real wealth to OPEC. Instead they chose to borrow to finance current consumption. They often spent the money unwisely, such as for subsidizing utility, food, and housing costs. Finally, they erroneously assumed that debt could always be refinanced or rolled over and therefore did not adequately manage the maturity structures of their debt and the debt-servicing requirements.

Bankers, too, made mistakes. Eager to lend, they fell into shortsighted competition and accepted clearly inadequate spreads. By too often focusing on front-end fees to increase current earnings and ignoring the total rate of return over the life of their loans, they bid the rates down to a level that did not adequately reflect the risk involved.

Finally, creditor governments share some blame because they turned a blind eye toward—or even encouraged, in the case of petrodollar recycling—the practices just described. The environment of the 1970s could not continue, and the 1980s brought rapid and dramatic changes.

Inflation rates declined dramatically. The rate of growth in consumer price indexes in the United States and other OECD nations fell from 13 percent in 1980 to 3.7 percent in the United States and 5 percent for the OECD countries in 1983. Oil prices declined significantly. Interest rates fell, but the real rate of interest rose from negative levels in the 1970s to near a positive 5 percent today. Countries that had borrowed on the thesis of negative real interest rates rapidly came to bear the full burden of their debts.

Furthermore, the world suffered the longest and deepest recession since World War II, causing LDC commodity exports to fall dramatically. Nonfuel commodity prices dropped 20 percent during the 1980 to 1982 period, while volume also decreased or stagnated. Thus, at the very time when debt-servicing burdens were escalating, the developing countries' sources of hard currency earnings were evaporating. The situation was untenable; the debt problem, inevitable.

Phase I:
Liquidity Squeeze,
Crisis Mentality

For some time, the U.S. Treasury and Federal Reserve had been concerned about the LDC debt situation. Throughout the spring and summer of 1982, these agents increased their monitoring activities. For example, they held a number of meetings with Mexican financial officials throughout 1981 and 1982, and requested, but never received, in-depth analyses and consultations with Mexico's Lopez-Portillo Administration in spring 1982. In addition to Mexico, the Treasury and the Fed were also keeping a close eye on the Argentine debt situation as a result of the Malvinas conflict.

Phase I of the debt problem is usually dated as beginning on Thursday, 12 August 1982. On that day, Mexico's then recently appointed finance minister, Jesus Silva-Herzog, called the Treasury to say that Mexico would completely exhaust its foreign exchange reserves by the following Monday. The next day, the Mexican finance minister was in Washington, D.C. Over an intensive weekend, the U.S. government arranged to prepay $1 billion for oil shipments to the Strategic Petroleum Reserve and provide $1 billion to Mexico in Commodity Credit Corporation (CCC) guarantees. The Treasury, the Federal Reserve, and the BIS agreed to bridge loans totaling $1.85 billion. Mexico squeezed by, but a crisis mentality developed almost immediately.

International confidence in the ability of the largest developing countries to service their debts had been dealt a staggering blow. With its vast oil reserves, Mexico had been considered among the most credit worthy of the LDCs. Within three weeks, the financial world was shaken again by similar problems in Brazil and Yugoslavia. In Argentina, the economic situation continued to deteriorate. By February, some 15 countries had encountered severe debt-servicing problems, involving moratoria, extraordinary financing, and forced reschedulings.

In retrospect, Phase I can be distinguished by the following factors:

Extreme liquidity problems for the debtors: Although their long-term economic prospects continued to be positive, the sudden constriction of international lending caused a major shortage of hard currency for many developing countries. The rollover assumption was shattered.

An atmosphere of impending crisis: Genuine fear of a collapse of the banking system and subsequent collapse of trade and a worldwide depression permeated the financial community. Although these fears were overblown and exaggerated by a press that did not comprehend the intricacies of the negotiations, it is difficult to overstate the morose atmosphere at the Toronto IMF/World Bank Annual Meeting in September 1982.

A global lack of experience in dealing with such problems: Financial institutions and government leaders had not dealt with problems of this magnitude and number. No one fully understood the nature or dimensions of the problem. Even so, through the leadership of the U.S. monetary authorities, the IMF, the BIS, and the cooperation of commercial banks and other creditor governments, disaster was avoided. Perhaps most important, the experience showed us that while the system was stretched thin at times, it could and did respond in rational, predictable ways.

Phase II:
Coming to Terms with
the Challenge

By February 1983, the monetary system had reached the brink and was coming back; Phase II had begun. Substantial progress had been made in settling some of the financial problems of key LDCs, and the international financial community's knowledge and understanding of the debt problem had increased dramatically. Confidence had been restored that the world's financial system would not collapse immediately.

Financial arrangements for the largest debtors were coming together by this time. Mexico's IMF program had been negotiated, and their bank package was assured by late December 1982. Argentina signed an agreement with the IMF in January 1983, and Brazil signed in late February. Although these latter two programs would need to be reworked later, they established at least a temporary stability. Yugoslavia completed an important package in February.

Equally important to the progress with individual countries was an early IMF Interim Committee Meeting (previously called for by the United States) that was held in February 1983. The Interim Committee agreed to an accelerated schedule for an increase in each member's IMF quota.

At the same time, the Group of Ten agreed to the U.S. proposal to modify and expand the IMF General Agreement to Borrow. This agreement was designed to serve as a standby borrowing arrangement for the IMF in emergency situations that might threaten the stability of the system. For the first time, there would be something of a safety net for the international financial system.

Also, by February 1983, a process for handling the debt problems involving the IMF, the BIS, creditor governments, bank regulators, bank advisory groups, and debtor governments had emerged. Finally, confidence had been restored. Most of the world's financial experts agreed that there would be no collapse of the world's financial and banking system. Only the press continued to predict such dire consequences.

The most significant characteristic of Phase II of the LDC problem was the establishment of IMF programs and financial arrangements with the debtor nations. A few smaller countries completed IMF standby arrangements in the last quarter of 1982, but most of the standby extended fund arrangements were established in Phase II. Since January 1983, IMF programs have begun for 33 countries, and 14 countries have completed rescheduling agreements.

Phase II can be further characterized by a succession of country-specific or minicrises. Every deadline on every loan in every country has seemed to bring a new minicrisis. More country-specific problems have erupted around the quarterly performance reviews with the IMF (such as in the cases of Brazil, Argentina, Peru, and so on). But these are minicrises, not systematic threats. Each can be solved. In the years ahead, it is safe to predict that more minicrises will occur. Conditions change and bring new challenges and new minicrises, but they, too, will be managed.

The third characteristic of Phase II is the rise and fall of the notions of a debtor's cartel or calls for global solutions. Debtor countries have come to realize that each country's situation is unique and requires a unique solution. In addition, developing countries, especially newly industrializing ones, realize that their prospects for future growth are enhanced by continued cooperation with the industrialized countries and the banking community rather than by confrontation and acrimony.

Similarly, so-called global bailout schemes also emerged and then faded away during this phase. These schemes, like the debtor's cartel, failed to recognize the uniqueness of each debtor's situation and the importance of continued involvement and cooperation by creditor banks and governments on an individual basis.

Phase II taught the world a number of important lessons. It reaffirmed that the LDC debt problem is indeed a major liquidity problem, not a situation of economic collapse and political chaos. It reassured the world that there is some stability in the international financial system—that evolution, not revolution, in the monetary system is required. It showed that interbank funding is perhaps more resilient than at first thought and that free governments of the debtor nations do behave responsibly and in their own self-interest. Financial actors have seen that most bankers can and will behave responsibly and have learned something about the dangers of hastily conceived financial plans like that attempted in the first Brazil financing program. Perhaps Phase II can best be described as a learning experience by illustrating that the international financial system can work but that each workout program must be tailored to the individual country's requirements and capabilities.

Phase III:
Meeting the Challenge and
Working out the Problems

At the end of 1983, Phase II was coming to a close, and the transition to Phase III was occurring—a new beginning for the world financial system. This section examines this phase in some detail by discussing the transition to Phase III, the key components of a successful Phase III, external threats to the resolution, and the need for progress.

I see year-end 1983 as the transition to Phase III because the largest uncertainties have been resolved. The necessary additional resources have been secured for the IMF, and irrational restrictions that might have effectively terminated international lending have been avoided.

Let us look first at the IMF. The IMF announced at the beginning of December 1983 that 129 countries, accounting for 96 percent of the total quota increase, have approved their additional funds and that the quota increases will therefore be implemented. This will provide $33 billion in new resources.

Throughout the U.S. initiative, for the first time the General Agreement to Borrow has been modified to provide a safety net to the international financial system. If required for systemic threats, this agreement could provide up to SDR 17 billion beyond normal IMF resources to the IMF in emergency situations.

The second largest uncertainty in this scenario has also been removed. November 1983 witnessed the reform of international lending laws in the United States and a similar parliamentary debate in Germany. Revised administration guidance on international lending has been developed in Japan. These actions remove the possibility of overly restrictive legislation that would cut off future international lending. These new laws should curb excesses while they provide incentives for continued bank participation in restructuring existing debts and providing additional financing. In fact, additional disclosure and enhanced capital requirements will strengthen the banking system.

The components, or characteristics, of Phase III constitute the implementation of a five-point strategy plan as follows:

1. The adoption of policies by industrialized governments to promote sustained noninflationary growth,
2. The encouragement of sound economic policies within LDCs to allow them to live within their resources,
3. The strengthening of international financial institutions like the IMF,
4. The encouragement of continued commercial bank lending,
5. A continued willingness to provide bridge financing where necessary.

Point 1

Today we see that economic growth is strong. In the United States, the recovery is well established, with the U.S. economy growing at a real rate of about 6.5 percent in 1983, and a forecast rate of 4.5 percent in 1984.

Japan achieved a 4 percent annual growth rate in the second quarter and is continuing stronger than originally expected. Germany saw four quarters of improving growth in 1983, and the news from other countries is good. OECD Secretary General Van Lennep has said that overall OECD growth is likely to be well above 3 percent in 1983 and that 1984's growth should be over 4 percent.

The economic recoveries of the LDCs depend on their ability to increase exports to the OECD countries and to each other. Clearly, there must be sufficient worldwide demand for debtor country exports to enable them to reduce their debt-servicing ratios to manageable, sustainable levels. Recent studies by Morgan Guaranty, the Institute for International Economics, and others suggest that demand for LDC exports is in large part a function of OECD real economic growth rates. A key threshold for LDC exports is for the OECD growth rate to reach 3 to 3.5 percent. Given current OECD growth rates, this should occur. These data are consistent with internal U.S. government projections.

Most industrialized countries are revising their growth estimates upward. We are now seeing an upturn in key commodity indicators. For example, *The Economist*'s commodity price index has increased some 23 percent since the beginning of 1984. Thus, both the volume of LDC nonoil commodity exports and their prices have been increasing.

Point 2

At this time, the evidence on Point 2 is mixed. On the one hand, Mexico's performance has been exemplary. The IMF approved a revised Brazilian program adopted by the democratically elected Congress. The new government in Argentina assumed office on 10 December 1983, and it indicated its intention to adopt sounder economic policies to revive that economy. Korea has announced new policies to ensure that it maintains a suitable debt-servicing ratio.

On the other hand, of the 42 programs initiated over the past 15 months, 13 (or 31 percent) have faced temporary funding interruptions due to noncompliance. Thus, while two-thirds have proceeded without interruption, a number have had problems.

In general, I am hopeful that future progress will be smoother. The most difficult periods for any country occur at the beginning of economic adjustment programs. Expectations, past practices, and domestic politics must all be altered in relatively few months, but the benefits require time. We have seen that phenomenon in the United States. However, it is reasonable to predict that fewer problems will arise in the coming years.

Point 3

The IMF, as an example, has proven to the financial community that it has the capacity to meet the demands, both from a financial and managerial perspective. On the financial side, the IMF now has an improved balance of inflows and outflows. I have discussed the inflows, or new resources. Just as important, policies have been adopted that should match outflows to the level of resources. The debate at the 1983 IMF/World Bank Annual Meeting over the access formula resulted in the adoption of policies that will allow the IMF to keep a balanced book over the next few years.

The IMF should also be managerially capable of meeting the demands. Forty-two countries have initiated IMF programs over the last 15 months at the same time that the IMF was concentrating on quota increases and borrowing. Given that monitoring requires less managerial effort than initiating new programs, the executive board and fund staff are likely to be less stretched in the future.

Point 4

New lending and the refinancing of existing debt through rollovers and extension of maturities must occur. We have seen that so-called involuntary lending is a viable source of at least interim or temporary financing. This was recently demonstrated by the level of bank commitments to the $6.5 billion package for Brazil and the willingness of banks to roll over debts maturing in 1984.

The banking community realizes that the future prospects of most major debtor countries are bright and that it would be a serious mistake to jeopardize the soundness of the large volume of existing loans by refusing to make relatively small additional loans. Having said this, I expect that in Phase III banking syndication minicrises will continue as some banks attempt to remove themselves from international lending. In addition, long and extremely difficult negotiations over lengths of grace periods, tenor, fees, spreads, and other terms will continue to produce country-specific minicrises for the foreseeable future.

Point 5

The BIS has met, and continues to meet, its challenge by assembling multilateral bridging packages such as in the cases of Mexico and Brazil. Since August 1982, the BIS has assembled or participated in over $4 billion of bridging operations for key LDCs. The successful repayment of all these bridges again places the BIS in position to respond to future crises should they develop. I have confidence also that monetary authorities around the world in the creditor countries can and will meet any unanticipated challenge.

Conclusion

Under the conditions I have described, the debt problem should materially ease over the next several years. For example, analytical studies by the Institute for International Economics show the debt-servicing ratios of over 20 key debtors declining by an average of some 21 percent over the 1983 to 1986 time period. But this resolution of the problem depends on avoiding major external threats to the resolution of the LDC debt problem.

However, three major threats exist to resolving the problem: (1) protectionism, (2) a possible resurgence of high interest rates, and (3) potential oil price increases. It is within the industrialized nations' power to avoid protectionism. The record is mixed. The United States has been partially successful in resisting protectionism, but the House of Representatives recently passed disastrous domestic content legislation. There are increasing calls for an industrial policy and even a politically potent call for a fixed quota on imports of carbon steel. The U.S.-Japanese voluntary auto limitation has been extended another year. In Japan, the trend is in the right direction, but progress has been agonizingly slow considering their highly protectionist starting point. In Europe, the recent record has not been good, and calls for additional agricultural restrictions bode ill. Finally, the LDCs often contribute to the problem of protectionism by unfairly subsidizing their exports. Political pressure then builds to limit their exports to the developed countries.

I am not very concerned about increases in interest rates. Over time, pressure amounts for decreases in interest rates. U.S. interest rates are high in real terms considering that inflation is expected to remain low and U.S. monetary policy appears to be appropriate. Despite my optimism, I recognize that interest rates pose a serious threat. Each 1 percent rise in LIBOR adds $3 billion to the annual debt service of the LDCs and makes resolution of the problem that much more difficult. The United States in particular must pursue policies to lessen the pressure on U.S. interest rates.

Concerning oil prices, the outlook is reasonably favorable. Economist Michael Evans predicts that there is as much as a 50/50 chance that OPEC will be forced again to lower its oil prices. Salomon Brothers and a number of others have concurred in the view that oil prices may fall. Since September 1983, despite Iraq's new jets and Iranian threats against Gulf shipping, spot prices for foreign crudes have been $0.50 per barrel or more below long-term contract levels. The USSR, in November 1983, cut prices on its Ural crude by $0.25 per barrel. However, a steady lowering of oil prices is critical if we are to see an easing of the debt problem. Every $1 increase in oil prices costs the oil-importing LDCs some $1.3 billion per year in foreign exchange. Equally important, major oil price increases lower the industrialized countries' growth rates, causing reductions in LDC export prices and volume. They can ultimately result in higher inflation and lowered living standards.

On the whole, I am reasonably optimistic about Phase III. Some might suggest I am Pollyannish, but taking a longer view, I do see substantial progress. I believe Phase III will bring a resolution of the debt problem. This resolution will not occur at the same time for all countries, and graduation from the debt problem is likely to be at least a couple of years away for even those countries in the most favorable situations. I would suggest that a country's debt problem can be considered resolved when:

The country's debt service ratio is in a manageable, sustainable range for 2 to 3 years in a row;

There has been a resumption of voluntary lending, as evidenced by oversubscription or competition among banks for new financings;

An active convertible currency bond market exists for that country's debentures;

The central bank of the debtor country has adequate foreign exchange reserves to weather temporary (for example, 1-year) interruptions in loans from overseas sources;

The economy of the country has increased real per capita incomes for at least 2 years in a row.

Phase III may bring resolution of the debt problem, but progress in Phase III is not automatic. Developing countries must adopt policies that strengthen their position—for example, encouraging more direct foreign investment. Such investment improves their balance of payments, increases employment, and transfers technology to the developing country. Fortunately, some progress is being made in this area.

A second major constructive action that developing countries should take is to eliminate unnecessary export subsidies. These subsidies increase the country's external borrowing requirements by contributing to government deficits and lead to protectionist actions in the developed countries that ultimately reduce access to their markets. By contrast, over time a properly valued currency and natural comparative advantages will provide the necessary stimulus to increase most countries' exports. In an interdependent world, exporting developing countries cannot expect to pursue beggar-thy-neighbor policies unilaterally while being financed by the importing creditor countries that have the highest level of unemployment in a generation.

In addition, it is reasonable to anticipate that debtor countries will begin to develop special financial arrangements to overcome individual difficulties. For example, some countries may wish to utilize discounted prepayments for marketable commodities to balance seasonal or irregular cash flows. Others may wish to consider issuing bonds that are indexed against future currency devaluations or backed by future exports—for example, Argentina could use wheat. Still others may shift to bonds, the face value of which is tied to an export price. So-called petrobonds have been discussed for some time. Perhaps in time a Nigeria, Venezuela, or Mexico may consider issuing petrobonds to retire currently outstanding medium-term commercial bank debt. During the coming years it is reasonable to anticipate a wide variety of new and innovative financing ideas from the debtor countries.

Just as the debtors adapt, so must the crditors. There must be better understanding of the problem. Although I have made the distinction between liquidity and solvency, it is in fact too simplistic an analogy to describe the developing country debt situation. In addition, the ratios used to describe a country's health—for example, debt service to exports or debt to GNP—are also in themselves inadequate. Better dynamic analysis of the country's macroeconomic progress and the interrelationship of its prospects with the rest of the world is crucial. Fortunately, demonstrable progress is being made in this regard.

In addition, creditor banks must set aside adequate reserves against losses to insulate themselves from the predictable problems of individual borrowers as the world moves from minicrisis to minicrisis in the next several years. In addition, I would anticipate that banks and other financial intermediaries will increasingly swap existing loans with each other to avoid overconcentration. This rebalancing of bank portfolios to lessen concentration, recognize actual values, and manage the timing of recognition of paper and tax gains and losses will ultimately strengthen the financial system. Just as the world's reinsurers spread the risk of a hurricane or natural disaster beyond the primary writer of the insurance, so too will resyndication and dispersion of the international debt where it will be less concentrated also promote both stability and a willingness to restructure and lend the fresh money that will be required during Phase III.

Note

1. William R. Cline, *International Debt and the Stability of the Economy* (Washington, D.C.: Institute for International Economics, 1983), p. 21.

21
Adjustment Pressures: Elements to an Overall Solution

Robert D. Hormats

There are growing tensions within many of the developing countries that are in the process of undertaking stabilization programs. There are pressures that result from postponed investment, a cutback in social programs, declines in employment, and a variety of other problems such as net capital outflows and reversals in overall trade performance. These pressures are growing and will continue to grow even though the IMF has taken an extraordinary leadership role in the effort to hold the system together and to encourage countries to undertake stabilization programs.

This chapter discusses some of the pressures and provides some sense of direction in how to deal with them. There are several important historical elements to the problem. First was the move from relatively long-term largely fixed rate borrowing to relatively short-term, largely variable rate borrowing that occurred in the latter part of the 1970s and that has created a great degree of uncertainty. This move also has had a major impact on both the stock and the flow of lending as interest rates went up.

Second, there was the factor of increased nationalism in terms of the borrowing of individual countries, a greater degree of reluctance to depend on equity investment or direct investment, and a greater degree of willingness, or acceptance, of debt financing. This changed the risk reward factor rather considerably and made the impact of the rise in interest rates that did occur in the early 1980s that much greater.

In a number of countries, also, there were other structural problems, and these structural problems resulted in a substantial buildup in state-owned enterprises, particularly in Latin America. But other elements of the problem can be demonstrated when one looks at the difference between the impact of the oil price increases and the interest rate increases in Latin America versus other parts of the world.

It is true that in the Philippines there have been problems and a few isolated cases in other parts of the world. But generally the impact has been much greater on Latin America than in other parts of the world largely because many other countries—perhaps East Asia is the best example—have concentrated much more on making their economies more efficient and on competing in the world market. The Latin American experience has been much more inward looking in part because their economies were larger than those of East Asia and in part because there was a greater degree of import substitution due to a variety of social and political reasons that made it difficult to cope with the major shocks that hit the world economy.

The major risks today are as much political as they are economic. As countries squeeze their economies down and generate more exports, there is a growing ability to repay debt. That is only part of the equation, however, because when countries undertake or suffer net capital outflows and reduce their growth to increase their exports and to reduce their imports with an emphasis on the latter, there is a growing degree of political dissatisfaction.

It is true that one answer to the debt problem is net capital outflow. The real question is how extensive that net capital outflow is and for how long it can be endured. There are limits, however. We do not know, sitting in Philadelphia or New York or Washington, D.C., what those limits are. But there are limits, and they differ, perhaps, from country to country, and in many of the countries it is possible to see a buildup of resentment about these stringent policies.

When does that resentment lead to pressure for unilateral action? It may be a month from now in some countries. It may not be until a year or two from now in others. But if policies that lead to declines in employment and to continued prolonged and substantial net capital outflows are continued, there is bound to be serious political ramification. There will be pressures for unilateral action by some countries. There will be pressures for countries to say we have agreed to pay you X, but now because of the pressures that are under way in our countries, all we're going to pay you is X minus $200 or $300 million a year; that is, there will be a greater degree of pressure for unilateral actions as opposed to negotiated solutions.

Anyone who has been to Latin America recently and has talked to people, particularly in Brazil and a few other large countries, will understand that these pressures exist. They have to be understood and dealt with, and to put our heads in the sand and say things are going well, now that growth is occurring in the United States, misses the fundamental problems that are occurring in the United States.

The question is what to do about it. I do not think revolutionary new international institutions are the answer. First, no one knows whether or not they will work. Second, it would take a lot of time to put them together. Bretton Woods was put together by an American and an Englishman who spoke the same language, and it took 3 years.

Third, there is no political consensus in the United States today for any major degree of government involvement in restructuring loans or assuming the private risks and putting them in the hands of the national government. It simply is not going to happen. It took a long time just to get the IMF allocations through Congress, much less transferring a greater degree of risk to the U.S. Treasury from the private sector.

Fourth, there will be much discontinuity if the United States even starts talking seriously about new lending. The reason is that new lending, which is already very slow, would probably not occur since people would say, "If we're going to get some brand new deal, why should we be lending money at our risk? Maybe the government will take that risk off our hands if we wait a year or so."

It is important that the United States take the leadership role. But it is also important that Europe and Japan play positive supporting roles. True, the largest debtor countries are in the Western hemisphere, but it is also true that the U.S. banks only have, depending on the countries, between 30 and 40 percent of the exposure. European and Japanese banks also have a substantial exposure. It is also true that while Latin America is the largest U.S. trading partner, indeed the largest single developing country area trading partner for the United States, Latin American trade ties with Europe and Japan have expanded quite dramatically over the last decade. Latin America is also a very large market for European and, to an increasing extent, Japanese exports. There is a common interest in the problem that was demonstrated in the degree of unity behind the effort to deal with the problems of Mexico and Brazil.

While no single dramatic solution exists, many elements for an overall solution do exist. The first and the most central is the effectiveness of the role of the IMF. The debtor countries need to have access to the IMF in what is known as an enlarged access position; that is, the IMF needs the flexibility to provide a substantial sum of money to the Brazils and the Mexicos and the others that are going to need it. In order to get that money, the IMF is going to have to go to the private markets at some point.

The realistic outlook is that the IMF is going to have to do some borrowing on private capital markets, and it is imperative that the U.S., Western European, Swiss, and Japanese capital markets permit the IMF to do that.

There is some opposition to IMF borrowing on private capital markets, largely in the United States and Germany. However, when they realize that it is better to use and go through the IMF, there will be a greater degree of understanding of the importance of this borrowing that goes along with the need to supplement the enlarged capital access requirement. I think it is also important that the General Agreement to Borrow be supported as well.

The second element of the solution concerns the World Bank and the regional development banks. The World Bank net new flows to Latin America, just for an example, have been under $2 billion. Obviously, growth has been larger, and there have been major repayments of some of the loans. I think it is important that the World Bank be encouraged to speed up its lending and in particular to provide more money for central or structural adjustment lending. This is extremely important because while the IMF provides balance of payments money, it does not provide structural lending. That is the business of the World Bank, the IDB, the Asian Development Bank, and others. Structural adjustment lending is particularly important because what really caused the problems in Latin America, when you dig down deep and go past the immediate borrowing, was the fact that the structures of the Latin American economies was simply not competitive in a very competitive world. This is not true of all industries, all sectors, or all countries, but many countries of Latin America were not as internationally competitive as their counterparts in other parts of the world, particularly Asia. Even when the world economy was growing at a very rapid rate, Latin America was losing market shares to other parts of the developing world such as India, Pakistan, and particularly East Asia.

If Latin America is to take advantage of whatever growth does occur on the world economy, it has got to make a lot of its industries much more efficient and much more competitive than they are now. Otherwise, even a lot of growth in one country is simply not going to benefit the big debt Latin American countries to the extent that it should. Therefore, structural adjustment lending is particularly important to support the efforts of these countries.

Other things need to be done. One finds a great deal of uncertainty still surrounding private investment in developing countries, and it is the same degree of uncertainty that surrounds a variety of other financial-debt-related issues. Is the climate today that is so attractive to foreign investors going to change tomorrow? Are those people who are advocating foreign investment today going to be out tomorrow, replaced by a reassertion of an anti-foreign-investment mentality that will hurt those people who invested in Latin America? Will some countries allow people to hold their debt, to buy into corporations now as a way of shifting the burden from debt to equity? I do not know the answer to that. In some cases there has been some indication of an interest on the part of developing countries, but it is not a clear trend at this point.

Are there other opportunities for private investment? When one looks at the private sector in Latin America, one finds opportunities for some countries to open up to a greater degree equity investment and direct investment. This is going to take time, however, and is by no means a panacea, although it is a step in the right direction, even if it is a step that is going to take some time to reach fruition.

There is a desperate need in many countries of the world for spare parts, raw materials, and basic equipment. The Eximbank has been providing some substantial lines of guarantees for both Mexico and Brazil. This is helpful because many of these countries suffer because they simply cannot get financing for imported basic raw materials, spare parts, and equipment. The result is a slowed rate of production and a decreased ability to export. These lines of credit are desirable. However, other countries that are involved, other industrialized countries, should join with the Eximbank and put into place the same types of programs. It is all well and good for the United States to do this, but a multilateral effort of a parallel nature is extremely important.

Other things also can be done. More and more there is going to be an exploration of the desirability of some sort of commodity index bonds and much more experimenting with floating rate bonds. The World Bank is already looking into these bonds. There probably will be also some discussion on how to reduce the variability of World Bank–sponsored floating rate notes and bonds.

Commercial bankers clearly will be reluctant to return to lending to sovereign risks in the developing world. They will be very cautious for a rather sustained period of time. That degree of caution, while understandable, will be treated with a common effort to help to differentiate among the better risks and the less desirable risks.

I do not expect a big pickup in international trade in the near future because there is almost no prospect of a major round of trade liberalization in the industrialized countries or in the developing countries. Each accuses the other of being protectionist. Domestic politics in all countries and relatively high rates of unemployment press governments to avoid major liberalization and press for more import restrictions. However, we have got to build the groundwork now for such a round of negotiations, and it will have to be done very carefully. The worst thing that can happen is to sit down in an ill-prepared meeting and have it fail and then to go home and say that multilateral solutions do not work. The world is very close to a wholesale retreat to unilateralism and needs a major meeting to try to turn back the movement toward more restrictions.

I do not see that happening right away, but I do think that is the direction in which to move. Debt, after all, is deferred trade. If there is no opportunity for countries to increase the rate of trade, then the debt situation is going to be with us for a long time.

To conclude, let me repeat that the world has a major problem. It has done well in holding the system together and patching up the cracks, but it is a long way from patching up to a genuine solution of the problem. The basic participants of the game—the international institutions, the commercial banks, and the governments involved—have made an enormous effort to work together. The degree of cooperation on the debt issue is virtually unprecedented.

One has to use all the available institutional resources that are at hand today—the IMF, the World Bank, the various development agencies of the United States and the other industrialized countries, the Eximbank, and the continued flows from the commercial banks. Otherwise, the international financial scene will face some dire situations in the future.

Part VII
Overviews

22

The Global Financial Structure in Transition: Consequences for International Finance and Trade

Christopher McMahon

There are two main conclusions and three main concerns to be drawn from the previous chapters. First, there is reasonable confidence in a sustained noninflationary recovery of OECD countries from now on at a rate that might be sufficient for that recovery. Second, I would suggest that there is confidence that the world is through the crisis stage of the sovereign debt problems and that these problems can probably be handled from now on although they will certainly take time, perhaps a number of years. A lot of effort and ingenuity will be required.

Balancing those two conclusions, there are three causes for concern. One of these was over the mix of U.S. policy between fiscal and monetary policies and, in particular, about the prospect of structural U.S. fiscal deficits. Second, there was clearly a lot of concern about the extent of the real adjustment that has already occurred and, alas, will still be required in the major debtor countries. Chapters 8, 11, and 12 cited dramatic figures, figures of falls in income quite unknown to the industrialized countries, where the word *adjustment* is used with great frequency. The concern about this adjustment is not so much about the determination of the people in power and control but whether or not there are social, political, and economic tensions that may prove difficult for them to handle. The third area of concern is over the rising tide of protectionism that most people deplore and few people think is over or has even reached its zenith.

Two major underlying problems may have to be faced that perhaps have contributed to some of the concerns and that will have to be dealt with in the transition that lies ahead to a more orderly noninflationary world. First, there is the question of policy consideration, the extent and success of policy coordination among countries, and the extent to which failures in coordination are contributing and will contribute to problems. Second, there are the implications of the explosive growth in the power and sophistication of the financial markets over the last decade and for the decade to come.

In one sense, of course, there is a lot of policy consultation. An enormous number of forums exist, starting at the very top with the IMF, the World Bank, the Interim Committee, the Development Committee, the Group of Ten, the OECD committees, the BIS for the central banks, regional groups, regional banks, development banks, and a great network of phone calls and discussions. This network of continually meeting together does have a very important benefit in that a network of understanding, knowledge, and awareness exists that can be called on in a crisis. The result is that there is no question that the international community has shown it is very good at crisis management.

Once a country wants money, it gets all the consultation, surveillance, and discussion of its affairs that it can possibly handle. However, there is still a problem about policy coordination at the highest level concerning the most important policy questions among major countries. This is not a question of lack of consultation but of effective interplay and surveillance. To use a clearer word, the major countries have only limited leverage on each other. Such leverage always has been limited, but maybe in the present world, without the background of a framework like Bretton Woods or a single dominant country as was the case in the period before World War I, there is more of a problem now.

An effort was made both at the Versailles Summit and at the Williamsburg Summit to develop a kind of surveillance of the major five countries by the IMF. This effort is very much to be welcomed, but it is important to see how far it can, or does, in fact, go. What tends to be the case in practice is that there is a general agreement of surveillance in terms of intentions and in terms of the overall thrust of policy whereas, what is important is what actually is happening, what is the development of policies that affect other countries. Here we come to a practical case, that of the United States at present. The United States has a very firmly articulated policy to reduce inflation and develop sustainable noninflationary growth. It is reasonable to say that it has done very well. It has got inflation quite a long way down and is already leading the world out of recession with a very remarkable, well-established, and probably sustainable recovery.

The way the United States has done this, however, the mix of policies, perhaps loose fiscal and perhaps tight monetary policies, has had severe consequences for other countries. It has been particularly difficult for other countries because there has been a general consensus in the world, a consensus that was reinforced at Versailles and at Williamsburg, of an antiinflationary stance, which meant tight fiscal policies and firm monetary targetry with an expectation that the benefit of the restrictive fiscal policy would flow to those countries, if inflation came down, through lower interest rates. It has been the case that the opposite mix of policy has been followed by the United States, which has frustrated the major countries such as Germany, Japan, and the United Kingdom in their hopes for the lower interest rates.

That I think is an interesting example of how different policy mixes, even though the intention is the same, can be disturbing to the world. It is very difficult to imagine any kind of surveillance solving this problem.

The industrialized countries and the IMF give advice all the time to the LDCs. However, it is quite hard to envisage such advice being given with real backing to one of the major countries. It is hard to envisage officials from the IMF actually walking down Pennsylvania Avenue, calling at those various stops on the way before they finally get to Capitol Hill to discuss with the U.S. Congress and tell them what policy they should adopt.

It is inconceivable that that should happen, but of course, for many countries that is what happens. As a U.K. official, I am in a particularly good position to make this point because I represent one of the few developed industrialized countries that has had the trauma of having lost control of events and had the IMF come in and that has seen the political difficulties involved in getting what was necessary and what was indeed a very successful policy in the end. It is important to remember, if there is going to be any degree of real surveillance and coordination of the world's policies, that an incursion on sovereignty, which is quite hard for people even to envisage, let alone actually accept, is going to take place.

Let me add here that it is not that U.S. policy has on average over the years been worse than the policies of all the other major countries. Other countries have simply been fortunate enough not to be the major reserve center so that their mistakes—and there have been plenty of them—have not caused as much tension and as many cries of pain from the rest.

However, some possibilities might be open for improving the situation. Sometimes it may be possible to trade off policy goals at the highest levels. Both the Bonn Summit and the Tokyo Summit were examples of how some leverage was exerted because some benefit could be found for everyone.

Another approach may be that in certain countries, perhaps not the United States, administrators may be able to enlist foreign criticism to help. A very well-known device of the Italian Treasury is to use the armies of the IMF and the EEC in their fight against high-spending ministries.

Another possibility, which is being explored in the OECD, is to enlist the interest of one group of officials spread through the countries against officials in other ministries. This OECD committee, which is concerned with the finance people, treasuries, and central banks, is making an attempt against the protectionist tide to make contact with the trade people in various governments and is trying to put to them arguments and pressure as a general group in which we have more in common through all our countries than sometimes ministries at home have with each other.

A first and most essential step, if there is going to be more harmony among countries, is that each country should explicitly take into account external affairs, the external value of its currency, and its balance of payments in making its policy. Almost all countries have to do this; it is a fact of life. But it is a fact of life that the United States does not always need to do that, and their not doing it can be deleterious to the general international framework.

The second of the two main questions was the implication for the international framework and for all sovereign governments and central banks of the growth and power of financial markets. I ask the question, the serious question, whether in a certain sense finance has moved from being the servant to the master of the goods markets.

Certainly in many foreign exchange markets it is commonplace that financial flows dwarf goods and other services flows by the factor of many times. The present interest rate volatility stemming from extremely febrile markets has led to a great deal of interest rate volatility that serves no positive purpose but that does in fact tend to bring the whole system into some sort of disrepute. Indeed, deregulation, which is part of the cause of growth in the financial market's power, may have raised interest rates above what they would have been.

To some degree, the exchange rate volatility and, in particular, the long-run swings of misalignment of exchange rates that are easy to discern, at least with hindsight, have clearly been damaging. They are due in some part, at least, to the dominance of short-term capital flows. These flows have had bad effects possibly on the degree of investment in the world but almost certainly on the increase of protectionism—in particular, the long-run swings between the dollar and the yen, which seem to have had a ratchet effect on protectionism in both the United States and Japan.

It can also be claimed that the LDC problems, though they are very complicated, have perhaps been exacerbated by the kind of elasticity of response of the financial markets. There was an extraordinary euphoria when international banks were pushing the loans on a country until the moment was reached when there was suddenly a perception that all had gone too far. Then everybody tried to pull out and pick up the pieces. Another example is the flight of private capital from Mexico in the years before the crisis when, in numerical terms, the whole of the borrowing actually went out as a private capital outflow.

Finally, I think that the enormous deregulation and the liberalization of institutions , the cross-ownership of different kinds of groups that is now going on and that is unstoppable, contain the seeds of new forms of risks that are going to force supervisors to keep very much on their toes to have any means of firmly controlling it.

Something can be done, however, at least in the foreign exchange markets, by a greater degree of assertion of authority by the central banks and governments. A very difficult question is how much authority can be asserted in the markets. It is no use going against fundamental trends fruitlessly. However, sometimes in recent years, policy makers have swung too far into a rather naive liberalism, a feeling that the markets are everything and governments and central banks simply have to accept whatever the markets bring. On many occasions I think markets would welcome more of a lead, though it would need a great deal of skill and care to do it properly.

23
Debt, Finance, Trade, and the Prospects of the Developing Countries

Barry Herman

Background

Not very many years ago, the developing countries were for the most part demonstrating a strong capacity for economic growth. Even the severe global recession of 1975 caused only a brief pause in total growth of output that otherwise averaged over 6 percent per annum during 1970 to 1979. With rapidly expanding export and domestic markets, with oil price increases spurring the search for new energy supplies, and with the overall need to finance higher domestic investment and import levels, many developing countries provided very attractive opportunities to international capital markets. The degree to which the markets responded—particularly the commercial banks—is a well-known story.

With the turn of the decade, however, the situation in many developing countries soured, and by 1982, recession was virtually everywhere in the Third World. Some developing countries began to recover in 1983 while others sank further into crisis. Among the latter, there are few prospects for any quick return to earlier growth trends.

In fact, discussions at the Fifth International Monetary and Trade Conference repeatedly returned to the theme of the economic situation and outlook of those developing countries in crisis and their implications for international banking practice. The following sections of this chapter synthesize those discussions and draw the major implications from them. The basic argument, however, may be stated briefly.

Whatever the limitations of domestic policy in developing countries over previous years, their consequences were clearly revealed by the unprecedented and unexpected global economic difficulties of the early 1980s. However, what turned a difficult situation into a crisis, especially for many of the middle-income developing countries, was a withdrawal of major commercial bank creditors from further lending. Without a replacement source of foreign capital, adjustment to the new situation could be nothing but severe austerity. Moreover, while austerity might be one way to deal with a balance of payments crisis in the short term, it does not solve the necessary adjustment problem for the medium term.

In the present context, adjustment means the achievement of a sustainable balance of payments situation. For heavily indebted countries in particular, this means the ability to service their debt fully and on a timely basis. That, in turn, requires a more rapid export growth and larger capital inflows than are now forecast, as well as less-punishing interest rates.

The conclusion can be seen in different ways. One is that the current debt levels of some developing countries are simply not sustainable over the medium term under world economic trends and policies. Some of that debt will have to be jetisoned at some point. This case entails a world of slow economic growth, losses to creditors that need to be apportioned, and frustrated aspirations. Alternately, developing country production of tradable goods could be expanded far more than is now foreseen. This option, however, requires renewed growth of capital inflows and lower interest rates. It also requires foreign markets to cease seeking to prevent surges in imports of the kinds of goods developing countries produce competitively. This latter picture, in short, requires a willingness to implement new policies.

Austerity: The Developing Countries' Problem, Not the Solution

Authors from Africa and Latin America have underlined the serious impact that the recent world economic recession has had on their regions. Chapter 14 pointed to four consecutive years in which the output of the non-oil-developing countries of Africa as a whole grew by less than population. Each of these years also saw a fall in the terms of trade of this group of countries; that is, even larger quantities of exports have been needed to purchase a fixed basket of imports. The result has been a precipitous fall in levels of real income per capita, which to start with were very low. The economic difficulties that such trends induced might have been ameliorated had capital inflows risen over the same period. However, it was Mr. Ogunleye's estimate that the sum of official and private capital inflows to the non-oil-exporting African countries had fallen in real terms since 1980. The result was that the volume of imports stopped growing in 1980 and has been falling since, in some countries causing acute shortages of necessary goods.

In Latin America, beginning from a higher average level of economic development and long-run rate of growth, the world recession brought a much sharper overall fall in living conditions. Mr. Curtin noted in chapter 10 that in seven member countries of the IDB, the per capita output gains of a decade were eliminated by the end of 1982. He estimated that the number of countries in that condition had doubled by the end of 1983. Unemployment and underemployment levels had increased to 30 percent in some countries, while per capita consumption levels fell. As in Africa, import levels have been sharply cut back in the face of recession-related levels of foreign exchange earnings and falling capital inflows, the latter immediately tied up with the difficulty in servicing high debt levels at high real interest rates.

In Latin America, Africa, and more generally, across the Third World, economic recessions are rarely cushioned by unemployment insurance or other welfare benefits, as various authors observed. Recessions thus necessarily have a stronger impact on the people of these countries than on those in developed countries. Indeed, it may be added that the impact on lower-income people in the developing world has been even further accentuated by widespread cutbacks in government subsidies—especially for food and fuel—made necessary by fiscal austerity. A further widespread effect has been a fall in real wage rates often effected through domestic inflation rates that raced ahead of nominal wage increases. In Mexico alone, according to Mr. Gurria (chapter 12), real wages were estimated to have fallen by 30 percent in 1983. Although no further fall was expected for 1984, Mr. Gurria also warned that the government had a limit beyond which it could not ask people to sacrifice. Analogously, Mr. Pratini de Moraes (chapter 11) wondered whether it has paid for Brazil to endure its most rigorous recession of this century. For the developing world as a whole, as observed by Mr. Onitiri in chapter 10, "the impact of the recession had to be evaluated in terms of countless millions of people subjected to hunger, deprivation, and destitution as well as the loss of production capacity owing to the shortage of foreign exchange to import parts and components and the vital equipment . . . needed to maintain existing infrastructures."

Taken together, various statements made in this book point to one overriding factor inducing economic recession and crisis in these developing countries—namely, an acute and unanticipated shortfall in foreign exchange available for imports of goods and services. Thus, in reviewing the early 1980s, many authors pointed to the unexpected sharp fall in commodity export prices and the stagnation in world trade volumes as well as the unprecedented rise in interest rates on new and much of existing foreign debt. The slowdown in new capital inflows, and in some cases considerable domestic capital flight, especially since 1982 under uncertain economic and political conditions, meant that official foreign exchange reserves had to be rapidly depleted. At the same time, for the heavily indebted countries in particular, debt amortization requirements began to fall due in larger amounts while the awaited pickup in export earnings failed to materialize owing to the persisting world recession.

With hindsight, Mr. Leutwiler (chapter 1) and Mr. McNamar (chapter 20) discerned policy errors that, had they been avoided, might have left the developing countries (and their creditor banks) less vulnerable in 1983. Both authors accused many developing countries of having avoided policy adjustments at an early stage, choosing instead to build up debt levels to maintain the momentum of domestic growth and development programs. Indeed, some authors thought that the austerity conditions imposed by today's foreign exchange constraint had been made necessary in certain cases by previous policy weaknesses, mismanagement, and corruption.

In contrast, there were also many criticisms of developed country policies—above all, U.S. fiscal policy—suggesting that no group of countries has been able to master fully the art of economic policymaking. Furthermore, as will be discussed later, the austerity policies now in place in much of the developing world need not be sufficient to set these countries back on an adequate long-run development path or allow them to service their debts fully over the long run.

The point, it seems to me, is that at a time of changes in economic conditions that are expected to be long lasting, it is usually necessary to make economic adjustments that, in turn, require changes in economic policies and additional investment to put them into effect. The best known examples are the two sets of increases in oil prices in the 1970s, each of which engendered intensified efforts in both conserving and increasing domestic energy supplies. Implementing those efforts required considerable new investments and the mobilization of both domestic and foreign resources to finance them.

In contrast, it is sometimes most efficient not to change policies in response to economic developments that are expected to be temporary. For example, shortfalls in export earnings arising from commodity price cycles or recessionary conditions in major markets may appropriately be financed rather than allowing import flows to be unduly disrupted. Indeed, for two decades the IMF has operated the CFF to help address precisely this problem.

In this context, one might say that many developing countries mistook certain long-run economic changes for temporary short-term ones. First, a major policy error made early in the present crisis by a number of developing countries was to misconstrue as a temporary change what now seems to be a long-lasting shift in real interest rates from zero or negative rates in the late 1970s to significantly positive real rates since then. The need to make severe cutbacks in externally financed fiscal deficits was accepted, however, by 1983. Achieving a more efficient use of capital in production will take much longer: the existing capital stock cannot simply be dismantled and reassembled in a form that better fits a new factor-price situation. It will take time for large capital-intensive projects with long payback periods to be deemphasized relative to other forms of investment.

Second, the stagnation in the growth of world trade was not expected to last as long as it did, and even today it is highly uncertain whether world trade will ever recover its earlier long-run dynamism. In a world of more slowly growing trade, countries can much less afford to become high-cost suppliers. Certainly, many developing countries have altered their view of how to manage their exchange rates for foreign currency in the last few years, accepting greater exchange rate fluctuation and allowing the effects of exchange rate changes to be passed on to domestic prices more readily. However, as observed by Mr. Hormats (chapter 21), for devaluation to stimulate import-competing and export-oriented sectors successfully requires increased investment expenditures.

The adjustments thus far described as necesasry in the present situation relate on the one hand to new investment requirements and on the other hand to economic management—for example, with respect to government expenditure, taxation, and pricing by public sector enterprises, as well as exchange rate policy or, more generally, getting the appropriate price signals. Austerity is not a requirement per se; it results rather from the sharpness of the adjustments owing to the sharpness of the shortfall in usable foreign exchange and the inability to shift domestic production quickly into exports and import substitutes. In this regard, Mr. Gurria characterized Mexico's recent adjustment experience as having been formed by easy access to external financing at first, followed by too little access later. A more appropriate balance, in his view, would have entailed sufficient finance to allow adjustment to take place over a measured period so that a minimum of economic growth and welfare could be maintained.

The role of the IMF in helping to promote such adjustment was recognized by a number of authors. That role entails both discussions of policy measures with governments and helping to enhance external financial flows, traditionally, by providing the IMF credits directly and recently also by marshalling private bank loans in certain cases. However, the IMF programs have not made provision for sufficient resources to avoid resort to stringent austerity programs. Indeed, the ability of countries to operate under the IMF adjustment programs has been mixed. As noted by Mr. McNamar, of the 42 IMF programs initiated over the 15 months ending in November 1983, almost a third have faced temporary interruptions of IMF lending due to noncompliance with performance criteria established as time-bound adjustment targets. According to Mr. Finch (chapter 9), a particular disappointment has been the accelerating rates of inflation in various developing countries. To a certain degree, it seems, this acceleration reflects the inflationary pressures of substantial exchange rate devaluations and cutbacks in price subsidies and illustrates the political as well as technical difficulties countries often have in controlling the expansion of domestic money and credit. It is understandable, while not laudable, that the pressures on governments to appropriate real resources through inflation would be strong when the total level of resources is unexpectedly cut back.

The developing countries are being urged—in this book as well as in numerous other forums—to learn to live within their resources. This was being done in some cases in a controlled and in others in a chaotic manner. Also, as it became clear that individual countries were not able to service their foreign debts, it has been impossible to reschedule them in conjunction with an economic adjustment program. However, the flow of new resources has largely disappeared. In a number of countries, as observed by Mr. Pratini, this process of adjustment under austerity coincides with—and perhaps unduly strains—an important transition to full democratic institutions.

The ultimate point, it seems, is that such adjustment under austerity may fail in the long run from the perspectives both of the people of the developing countries and their foreign creditors and investors; that is, even if sound fiscal management and prices that reflect real costs and profit opportunities are achieved, they need not necessarily lead to resurgent growth. But resurgent growth is needed both to raise living standards and to service foreign debts fully. Thus, according to Mr. Curtin, Latin America's adjustment "can be expected to result in either stagnation or moderately slow growth in the medium term after recovery." A central reason lies in what has happened to investment during adjustment. For example, after doubling in real terms from 1970 to 1980, Latin American investment rose 2 percent in 1981 and then dropped 13 percent in 1982, and a further fall, affecting all 24 countries of the region, was estimated for 1983.

The Unsatisfying Outlook for Foreign Capital Flows

The preceding discussion suggests that if the developing countries that have been forced to endure a period of austerity are subsequently to recover a significant rate of economic growth, then they will need sub-stantial net infusions of foreign exchange. Given the debt-servicing ob-ligations of many of these countries, they will need even larger gross foreign exchange increases that, in any case, can only come from ex-panded export earnings and capital inflows. Any increases in interest rates in major capital markets that raise the interest cost of the floating rate component of total foreign debt only exacerbate the problem.

A preliminary concern—at least from the viewpoint of the interna-tional creditors of the countries with relatively high debt levels—is the extent and speed of improvement in the overall debt-servicing capacity of these countries. Certainly, it is not widely expected that there would be any large-scale new autonomous private credit flows to the heavily indebted countries in advance of a subtantial improvement in measures of their debt servicing such as the ratio to foreign exchange earnings of total foreign interests and amortization payments. The numerator of that ratio depends on original and rescheduled obligations of all debtors in a country and movements in the base interest rate (usually LIBOR or the U.S. prime rate) that is used to calculate the interest cost of the floating rate portion of total debt. The denominator of the ratio depends on the degree of success in expanding export earnings. Given a slow growth outlook in the oil-exporting countries that had served as a dy-namic pole for world growth over the previous decade, the outlook for export expansion effectively reduces the outlook for expansion of in-dustrialized country imports.

Perhaps the most optimistic view, in this regard, was that of Mr. McNamar, who saw U.S. economic growth surging at above 4.5 percent in 1984 and who cited recent estimates of the OECD that growth of the OECD countries as a whole would be over 4 percent in 1984. Such growth might substantially increase demand for developing country ex-ports, helping to boost the prices of primary commodities as well as in-creasing trade volume overall. However, many of the other authors were at least implicitly taking a wait-and-see approach; that is, whether or not such OECD growth would be sufficient to draw in developing country exports in adequate amounts remained to be seen, particularly given the surge in developed country protectionism in recent years in-volving many goods that the developing countries wished to export. Certainly, the opposition was clear to unrestricted imports in the United States of steel made in the developing countries, as voiced by Mr. Boni (chapter 17). Indeed, numerous authors, including Mr. McNamar, ex-pressed their concern about widespread protectionist tendencies' af-fecting world trade in general and developing countries in particular.

A further concern in the debt-servicing outlook was the prospect for interest rates. All authors who addressed the issue expected high U.S. and thus Euromarket real interest rates to continue into the foreseeable future, albeit for a variety of reasons. Mr. McNamar, expecting U.S. inflation to remain low, saw pressures for nominal interest rates to fall. The opposite view, however, appeared to be more common. In fact, this latter view was seen as characterizing the U.S. financial market at the end of 1983; for example, Mr. Pardee (chapter 5) saw the expectation of higher future interest rates as one of the factors accounting for the steep yield curve—that is, long-term interest rates that were high relative to short-term rates.

One major source of concern over interest rates related to the combination of high prospective U.S. government budget deficits and monetary policies that aim to contain inflationary pressures. The recessionary implications of such a scenario led Mr. Leutwiler to warn that "it would be dangerous, however, to assume that we are about to enter an era of high and sustained (OECD) growth."

The authors did not consider explicitly the degree to which, all in all, the debt-servicing ratio of the developing countries was likely to improve. Nevertheless, data available on trade and capital flows at the time of writing suggest that a significant improvement in developing country exports had begun in 1983 while there was only an extremely small increase in net lending to these countries. Interest rates, however, were on the march upward again. The net effect is that there should be some improvement in the debt-servicing ratio in 1984 compared to that in 1983, especially if interest rates do not rise much above their May 1984 levels and if certain surplus oil-exporting countries remained willing, as reaffirmed at the end of 1983, to restrain their oil production, thereby permitting an expansion in oil exports from other producers.

It is not possible to say with sufficient assurance that debt-servicing ratios would continue to improve in 1985, and they should significantly deteriorate thereafter, especially as rescheduled amortization payments begin to fall due, particularly in 1987. If those banks that Mr. McNamar saw as still attempting in 1983 to remove themselves from international lending instead had more confidence, they would probably be less likely to provoke the "syndication minicrisis" that he expected would continue. Certainly, the attitude expressed by authors from some of the larger U.S. banks reflected their continuing apprehension. As one executive from a large U.S. bank put it, most large banks that were already substantially exposed in high-debt countries were probably not willing to extend their lending voluntarily in the near term. The best that should be hoped for, he suggested, was for the IMF to mandate, in effect, a yearly private lending program for these banks within the context of ongoing adjustment programs for the countries in question.

Indeed, the debts of the large debtor countries are so large and their capital import needs are so great that no other source of finance, public or private, was a practical substitute for international bank finance. Thus, some accommodation with the banks had to be achieved. This might be seen as muddling through, but no one seems interested in implementing any of the radical proposals for debt reform and reduction by which, for example, some independent authority would buy up developing country debt at a discount from the banks. Mr. Hormats (chapter 21) expressly opposed such schemes on three grounds: first, negotiations to create them would necessarily be very long and difficult; second, there was not even a political consensus that the government should have a role in assuming what is now the debt-servicing risk of private banks; and third, the adoption of a scheme that imposed losses on banks would probably stop new lending at least until the outcome of negotiations to establish such schemes was known.

In any event, there was little evidence that net bank lending to the developing countries, especially by U.S. banks, would return to buoyant growth rates any time soon. This is not to deny that some bankers saw fresh bank funds being provided for export and project finance, the latter especially in conjunction with so-called cofinancing schemes as operated by the World Bank and the regional development banks. In fact, it may be added, in September 1983 the World Bank approved its first loan under a new cofinancing instrument for use with commercial banks. Nevertheless, it was at least the experience of the IDB, as reported by Mr. Curtin in chapter 10, that it was currently difficult to mobilize funds for IDB cofinancing under perceived risk levels. This was despite the fact that with cross-default clauses there has never been a case of default on IDB loans, at worst only short-lived delays in payments. He thus did not see a prospect for much growth in cofinancing for the time being.

In a similar vein, Mr. Hormats saw a high degree of caution and selectivity among bankers with respect to further sovereign risk lending. He did, however, foresee possible experimentation in the bond markets—for example, with floating rate bonds and commodity-backed bonds. So-called petrobonds had been discussed for some time. Similarly, Mr. McNamar also saw debtor countries considering discounted prepayments for marketable commodities as a form of finance for seasonal or irregular cash flows or, for longer-term finance, bonds indexed against future currency devaluations as well as export-backed bonds.

Cognizant of the dampening effect on the perceived high-risk levels on private sector lenders, Mr. McNamar pointed to certain factors that should lessen the degree of uncertainty. First, the resources at the disposal of the IMF for lending to countries with balance of payments needs had just been raised through approval of an IMF quota increase and the newly expanded and liberalized General Agreement to Borrow.

Second, reform of international banking regulations was now well underway in the United States, the Federal Republic of Germany, and Japan, and it was becoming clear that while new legislation should curb excesses, it would also provide incentives for continued and enlarged financing. Third, a point made as well by Mr. Finch of the IMF (chapter 9) and Mr. Leutwiler of the BIS, the experiences of 1982 and 1983 showed that the international monetary system was responsive to crisis conditions and would remain so. Finally, another point might be added—namely, that despite the recent international crisis, banking profits had improved, thus providing an opportunity for banks in a number of countries to make substantial additions to loan-loss provisions. More generally, banks have been encouraged by their government supervisors to strengthen their capital-asset ratios through increased retained earnings. Their situation is in this sense less weak than it had been, for example, in mid-1982.

These factors notwithstanding, a considerable residual degree of riskiness appears to be constraining net private sector capital flows to the developing countries. By the same token, due to remaining uncertainties about the outcome of adjustment policies as well as the net availability of foreign credit, it may not prove possible to attract quickly back to the developing countries all the domestic flight capital that had left over the recent past. Concerning the Mexican case, for example, Mr. Gurria observed that a painful lesson was learned concerning the cost of maintaining an overvalued exchange rate and uncompetitive domestic interest rates. He felt that the planned steady devaluation of the peso vis-à-vis the U.S. dollar, along with higher Mexican interest rates, would help to restore confidence. However, he continued, it would take time as investors waited to see if Mexico had the political will to maintain a consistent policy over an extended period.

An area of uncertainty pertaining to the IMF and the debtor countries in general also seems to remain; that is, despite the new resources provided to the IMF, it is not clear whether the fund will be willing to commit sufficient resources to individual borrowing countries if the need arises, owing to the decision of the IMF Executive Board not to expand country borrowing limits in 1984 and to consider reducing them for 1985. Thus, Mr. Hormats advocated continuation of the Enlarged Access Policy of the IMF when the question of extending it arose at the autumn 1984 IMF Interim Committee meeting. He also considered that the IMF may eventually have to obtain additional resources through private market borrowings. The latter, he argued, would be obtainable at extremely attractive terms since, among other factors, the IMF could back its borrowings with its stock of gold worth approximately $40 billion. Conversely, Mr. Finch felt it was unlikely that the IMF would be given the authority to go to the market to increase its lendable resources.

If the outlook for private credit flows to the developing countries was perforce to remain restrained, the outlook for other types of capital flows to these countries varied from uncertain to weak. Private direct investment, for example, was pointed to by numerous speakers as a hopeful source of foreign capital. Mr. Leutwiler, for one, also saw it as a possible means of reducing the debt burden of the heavily indebted countries; that is, he thought the suggestion worthy of consideration that countries with large endowments of natural resources or profitable state-owned enterprises might sell some of these assets to their creditors. More generally, different speakers referred to a strong increase in the role developing countries have recently been ready to accord to direct foreign investors as reflected in their more liberal investment incentive policies and the actual recruitment efforts of a number of them.

It seems that there are reasons not to be overly sanguine about direct investment flows over the medium term. First, in many cases, the interest of developing countries is to attract firms that will help boost exports that may be of the type that might come up against protectionist barriers in the corporation's home country. Moreover, for countries expecting an extended period of austerity, local market prospects might not be sufficiently attractive for the time being to warrant investing. Second, as observed by Mr. Hormats, no matter how attractive incentives may be, they can be changed after investments are made and conditions ease so that some policy uncertainty remains. Third, as Mr. Onitiri (chapter 13) remarked, in the countries that make up the poverty belts of Asia and Africa, and especially in the LDCs, there are major deficiencies in critical economic and social infrastructures that are not amenable to amelioration through direct foreign investment. Indeed, creation or improvement of publicly financed infrastructures such as roads, posts, and utilities are often preconditions for attraction of direct foreign investors, as observed by Mr. Ogunleye.

Foreign financial support for infrastructure projects—both in the narrow bricks-and-mortar sense and in the human capital sense of education, public health, and technical assistance—has traditionally been the province of official development assistance (ODA) and long-term credits extended through the multilateral official financial institutions. As observed by Mr. Ogunleye, ODA trends have been quite disappointing, especially measured against the United Nations aid target of 0.7 percent of GNP, which many developed countries have adopted as their national policy goal. Singling out the United States, Mr. Leutwiler deplored its intention to reduce certain modes of concessional economic assistance at this time. Indeed, almost simultaneous with the Global Interdependence Center conference, the United States—in what *The New York Times* editorialized as "America's hurtful parsimony" (8 December 1983)—was rejecting appeals by 31 of the world's richest countries to raise the amount it was willing to contribute to the International Development Association (IDA), the highly concessional facility of the World Bank. The IDA, it should be noted, supplies funds exclusively to the poorest countries of the world (with per capita incomes up to $400 a year), most of which have at best only very limited access (or ability to service) private foreign credit.

Although lending by the World Bank and the regional development banks is primarily project oriented, these institutions have also engaged in broader program lending that various authors in this book wish to see further expanded. As observed by Mr. Ogunleye, in Africa especially, such lending serves to lessen stringent constraints on imports. In a related vein, Mr. Curtin described how the IDB is providing finance in Latin America on a limited basis and for a limited period for the purchase of imported inputs to permit industrial reactivation of underutilized plant capacity for manufactured exports. In addition, Mr. Hormats advocated speeding up the resource flows under a specific type of World Bank program lending—namely, structural adjustment lending. As the name suggests, such lending supports the balance of payments position of a borrower while various policy reforms are implemented that are aimed at the sort of long-run balance of payments adjustment discussed in the preceding section.

A remaining source of financial flows to the developing countries discussed here was officially supported export credits. As described by Mr. Draper (chapter 4), the outlook was favorable for expanded Eximbank flows, or more particularly for guarantees of loans actually provided by the banking sector. Although direct Eximbank credits are sometimes provided, they are less highly subsidized than they had been, and in fact, all subsidies are to be removed by July 1986 under new OECD guidelines. Although Eximbank guarantees are available for exports to most countries, Mr. Draper described a new $1.5 billion facility that was recently established specifically for exports to Brazil in response to the similar facility for Mexico that was also under preparation. Citing this approach approvingly, Mr. Hormats suggested that the other OECD countries should join in efforts comparable to this U.S. effort.

Taking all the sources of capital flows together, there do not seem to be grounds for optimism on the degree to which the developing countries will be able to import capital under current private sector risk assessments and public sector policies. No attempt was made by the contributors to estimate by how much capital flows to the developing countries might grow—a necessarily highly conjectural exercise. Nevertheless, it is suggestive to compare reasonable orders of magnitude for prospective real growth rates over the next 5 years with the experience of the 1970s.

First, economic aid flows, which grew by over 7 percent per annum in real terms in the 1970s, are likely to grow at roughly a 3 percent real rate as the factors that accounted for the higher earlier growth rate recede; that is, neither oil-exporting countries nor the high-donor developed countries are expected to be in a position to raise their aid effort as a share of GNP, and a further fall in the relative U.S. aid effort is quite possible. Second, nonconcessional official flows (mainly regular lending through the World Bank, regional and other development banks, and official export credit institutions), which grew by about 13 percent a year in the 1970s, should probably not be projected to grow at a rate above that of the first 2 years of this decade—that is, almost 7 percent annually. Third, net private direct investment, which grew almost 8 percent per annum in the 1970s, especially on the strength of investment in services as well as in the more traditional manufacturing sector, is considered in various studies to be likely to grow now in the range of 3 percent a year, given lower expectations for developing country growth in output and trade. This leaves private credits (primarily international bank and bond finance), which grew in the 1970s by around 11 percent per annum in real terms. In nominal terms, a pessimistic assumption would be that there would be no net private lending, while perhaps an optimistic case would be to extrapolate the 7 percent projection for 1983 and 1984 made by the managing director of the IMF.

All these projections, taken together, imply a total average annual growth of real capital flows of up to about 3 percent. For the 1970s, in contrast, the growth of net capital flows to the developing countries averaged about 9.5 percent. Thus, unless one believes that the developing countries will be able to increase their exports by quite buoyant amounts, these projections entail rather sobering implications for the development aspirations of the developing countries over the next half-decade.

A major precept of economic efficiency is that economic units—individuals and firms—should be able and willing to make adjustments to changing economic conditions. A plethora of protectionist actions is a symptom of a breakdown in that ability or willingness; it indicates a loss of confidence in market signals for resource reallocation. However, with persisting disequilibrium exchange rates, widespread subsidization, and quantitative restrictions on trade and production for so many goods and services, it is not clear how reliable market signals are. Free traders may bravely urge abandonment of all market interventions, but with so many people's livelihood at stake, it is no wonder that there is no large constituency for that, certainly at a time of high unemployment. But it is desirable to move toward a more productive economy, one in which people are fully and efficiently employed in making goods and services for domestic use and export in return for goods made more efficiently elsewhere. Getting to that position apparently may require some form of national industrial and agricultural policy tied to an internationally agreed rationalization and phased reduction in the management of trade.

Many might consider it preferable if no such planning were needed. For example, if growth in the industrialized countries were to surge ahead at a sustained and accelerated rate, it might be politically possible simply to dismantle protectionist barriers. The industrialized countries could then become a more dynamic growth pole, resolving the financial problems of the developing countries and recharging the growth of the latter through a rapidly rising demand for their exports. The only problem is that such an optimistic growth forecast does not seem realistic. On the contrary, world growth would be higher if trade were freer. In fact, if developing country debts are to be fully serviced as a whole, it will be necessary to return to a period of increasing integration of the world economy whereby world trade grows significantly more rapidly than world output.

Trade—The Long-Run Key to Finance, and Finance—the Short-Run Key to Trade

A number of proposals have been made, some at a large scale of international reform, that aim to improve upon the unsatisfactory outlook for the financial and trade flows outlined here. Contributors have mentioned a number of them, including the Integrated Program for Commodities, under negotiation at the United Nations Conference on Trade and Development since 1976, the recommendations of the Brandt Commission, and the 10-year recovery, reconstruction, and development transfers to the developing countries and stabilization of commodity prices, as suggested by Mr. Onitiri. Whether or not any of these proposals is on the road to implementation, as a group they entail an important insight—namely, that trends in international trade and finance are mutually reinforcing.

In the short run, trade would be promoted by a relaxation of the external financial constraint on the developing countries. As it is, limitations on the imports of the latter not only rob the developed countries of a demand stimulus to output but also reduce the capacity of the developing countries to undertake more export-expanding investments. In addition, at the time of writing, high and rising interest rates on foreign debt are absorbing large amounts of foreign exchange earnings that would otherwise be available for purchase of imports. The situation has been deteriorating to such an extent that a number of people, including the chairman of the board of governors of the Federal Reserve System, began discussing in mid-May the introduction of a ceiling on interest rates on developing country foreign debt. Developing country import capacity would also be enhanced by an expansion of foreign public credits extended to them. Even if political winds are against expanding such public flows now, these winds can change when the undesirable consequences of their present direction become clearer.

For the medium term, trade would be promoted by a successful new round of trade negotiations under the GATT. Undertaking such a round was advocated by Mr. Solomon (chapter 2). However, neither Mr. McNamar nor Mr. Hormats saw the political feasibility of such a Reagan Round in the short run. Indeed, reflecting back on the November 1982 Ministerial Meeting of the GATT, Mr. Hormats saw the unfortunate consequences of holding a high-level meeting that was not well prepared; that is, a groundwork of preliminary agreements was needed first, and that was precisely what had eluded the preparatory meetings in this case.

Certain recent experiences in negotiations restricted to the industrialized countries or even to different ministries within a single country have also been disappointing. Mr. Finch, for example, pointed to the contradiction between developed country finance ministers who seek to encourage developing country exports with which to service their debts and trade officials who act to stem the imports of these goods into the developed countries. Nevertheless, at least these groups of officials with contrasting responsibilities have begun to meet together in an international forum on a periodic basis. Mr. Ogunleye advocated, in effect, widening the joint trade and finance consultations into a North-South forum. This notwithstanding, Mr. McMahon did not see significant progress being made in the trade and finance coordination efforts already underway.

In fact, if there was one issue on which speakers from North and South and from official and private sectors agreed, it was that there would be no major successes in rolling back protectionism in 1984. The United States, in the midst of a long election campaign, would not make new initiatives, while the European unemployment situation would remain difficult. Indeed, exports from developing country plants financed with official international loans, like from the World Bank, could even become threatened by protectionist barriers, according to Mr. McNamar, solely owing to a subsidy element in the original loans. Mr. Boni, recognizing the dilemma as it affects the steel industry in the United States, recommended that some compromise be sought so that some steel imports would be permitted to help repay loans while still giving the U.S. industry temporary protection from lower-cost foreign producers.

The great unresolved question in steel, as well as in other sectors, is how and whether to produce such a compromise. One possibility is negotiation of a world steel agreement, controlling trade over a limited period, with an agreed schedule for phasing out the controls. By including all major producers, such an agreement would rationalize the patchwork of bilateral limitations of trade, the protectionist intentions of which were defeated when new exporters replaced the previous, restricted suppliers. Each country, in working out its negotiating position in such an endeavor, could presumably take into account the demands of steel consumers and banking creditors to the exporters as well as those of the steel producers.

Such an outcome would be an acknowledged departure from free trade that, in the view of various participants in the conference, was a myth anyway. Certainly, steel is not imported into the United States in 1984 under free market conditions. The questions then are: How long should steel remain unprotected? What are the guarantees that the steel industry will take adequate steps to become competitive by some target date? If U.S. steel cannot become competitive in a reasonable length of time, on what grounds should it be protected? Are they enough?

In conclusion, if debt is nothing but deferred trade, as Mr. Hormats suggested, and if international finance is nothing but a means of effecting an international movement of real resources, then the future of international finance is the future of international trade. The recent crisis in international finance arose largely from the effects of the recession on trade. The ultimate resolution of that crisis awaits a resolution of the trade problem. In the long run, there is no other way that foreign debt can be serviced and developing country growth be restored to more normal levels.

Index

About the Contributors

Robert E. Boni is president and chief operating officer of Armco, Inc.

Michael E. Curtin is executive vice-president of the Inter-American Development Bank.

William H. Draper III is president and chairman of the Export-Import Bank of the United States.

C. David Finch is director of the Exchange and Trade Relations Department at the International Monetary Fund.

Robert M. Gottschalk is an attorney-at-law and senior partner in the firm of Robert M. Gottschalk, P.C. He is the author of numerous articles on foreign affairs and international trade.

Angel Gurria is director, public credit, Mexico.

Barry Herman is economic affairs officer for the General Analysis and Policies Division of the Department of International Economic and Social Affairs of the United Nations. He is a contributor to the United Nations World Economic Survey and other U.N. publications on North-South economic relations.

William T. Hogan, S.J., has authored a number of books, including *Economic History of the Iron and Steel Industry in the United States.* He is a professor of economics and the director of the Industrial Economics Research Institute at Fordham University.

Robert D. Hormats is vice-president for international corporate finance and director of the International Corporation for Goldman, Sachs & Co.

Pedro Pablo Kuczynski is managing director and president of First Boston International. He has written extensively on Latin American economic affairs.

Fritz Leutwiler is chairman of the Governing Board of the Swiss National Bank and chairman of the Board of Directors and president of the Bank for International Settlements.

Christopher McMahon is deputy governor, Bank of England.

R.T. McNamar is deputy secretary, U.S. Department of the Treasury.

Shijuro Ogata is executive director, Bank of Japan.

Samuel A. Ogunleye is vice-president for planning and external relations, African Development Bank, Abidjan.

Herbert M. Onitiri is special advisor to the United Nations Development Program. He has published extensively in academic and trade journals on subjects ranging from economics and public policy to foreign aid and African development.

Scott E. Pardee is executive vice-president of the Discount Corporation of New York and a director of the firm's Board of Directors. He is also a director and member of the Finance Committee of American International Group, Inc.

John D. Paulus is principal and chief economist of Morgan Stanley.

M.V. Pratini de Moraes is a member of the Brazilian Congress representing the state of Rio Grande de Sul, president of the Foreign Trade Foundation, a member of the Advisory Council of the Center for Brazilian Studies, and a member of the Executive Committee of the Brazilian section of the Brazil/U.S. Business Council.

Jon W. Rotenstreich is treasurer of IBM Corporation and a director of the Torchmarch Corporation.

Anthony M. Solomon is president and chief executive officer of the Federal Reserve Bank of New York. In that post he serves as vice chairman and a permanent voting member of the Federal Open Market Committee.

Joseph Spetrini is director of the Agreements Compliance Division, Import Administration, of the U.S. Department of Commerce.

About the Editor

Joel McClellan is director of the Quaker United Nations Program in Geneva. Prior to this, Mr. McClellan was the European representative of the Global Interdependence Center, Geneva. He has been a professor of economics at the University of Singapore and the Chinese University of Hong Kong. He has written on international trade and agricultural development in Asia. He has an M.A. in economics from the University of Wisconsin.